Designer	Malcolm Smythe	© Aladdin Books Ltd	*First published in the*
Art Director	Charles Matheson		*United States in 1984 by*
Series Editor	James McCarter		Franklin Watts
Editor	Gregor Furguson	*Designed and produced by*	387 Park Avenue South
Researcher	John MacClancy	Aladdin Books Ltd	New York NY 10016
		70 Old Compton Street	
Illustrators	Nick May	London W1	ISBN 0-531-04867-5
	Rob Shone		
	Jim Robins	*Printed in Belgium*	Library of Congress
	Cooper-West		Catalog Card No. 84-51223

The publishers would like to thank the following organizations and individuals for their help in the preparation of this book:
Aerospatiale; Avions Marcel Dassault Braguet Aviation; British Aerospace; Boeing Military Airplane Corporation; CASA; Computing Devices Co Ltd; Ford Aerospace and Communications Corporation; General Dynamics Corporation; Hughes Aircraft Corporation; Interavia; International Defence Review; Israel Aircraft Industries Ltd; Martin Baker Aircraft Co Ltd; Martin Marietta; McDonnell Aircraft Company; M L Aviation Co Ltd; Office of Public Affairs, Airforce Systems Command; Plessey Group; R Alkan (UK) Ltd; Rolls Royce Ltd; Saab-Scania AB; Thomson-CSF and Thorn EMI Electronics.

Photographic Credits:
4/5 Office of Public Affairs, Air Force Systems Command; 6/7 General Dynamics; 10/11 Dassault Breguet, Grumman; 14/15 Boeing Military Aircraft Corporation; 16/17 C M Harvey; 18/19 Grumman; 20/21 The MacClancy Collection, General Dynamics; 22/23 Lockheed, Boeing Military Aircraft Corporation; 24/25 McDonnel Aircraft Company; 26/27 AEG Telefunken; C M Harvey, General Dynamics; 28/29 British Aerospace; 30/31 C M Harvey; 32M L Aviation, British Aerospace, Israel Aircraft Industries; 34 to 44 The MacClancy Collection.

20th CENTURY WEAPONS

COMBAT AIRCRAFT

CHARLES MESSENGER

FRANKLIN WATTS

New York · London · Toronto · Sydney

Introduction

It was a little over eighty years ago that the first "heavier than air" flying machine actually to take off from the ground was built. A few years later, at the beginning of World War I, combat aircraft appeared and added a new dimension to warfare. At first, military aircraft were used simply for spying on the enemy. Very quickly, however, they took on new roles. There were bombing aircraft, aircraft for controlling artillery fire, and fighters whose principal job was to attack other aircraft. The latter became very important, as it was soon realized that the side that had control of the air had more chance of winning the battle on land. Aircraft could attack the enemy with bombs and machine guns on the battlefield itself, and also strike directly at the enemy's country. Over the years, more tasks were given to aircraft in war, from patrolling the seas to transporting troops and supplies.

Today there are literally hundreds of different types of military aircraft. They range from light, fast fighters to huge bombers that can carry 30.5 tonnes (30 tons) of bombs; there are also aircraft that can carry over 100 paratroopers, and light bombers that can fly for hundreds of kilometers inside enemy territory at only 76m (250ft). All these, and more, are used by the world's airforces today.

Therefore, the term "combat aircraft" includes not just fighters, but bombers, ground attack aircraft, and surveillance and transport aircraft also. Used in its widest sense, it covers any aircraft with a war purpose.

This Book
Designed to show you the modern combat aircraft, this book covers its roles, how the aircraft is constructed, the engines, electronics and weapons systems, and aerial tactics. The crews who fly the sophisticated aircraft of today are discussed as well as how a military airfield operates. A section on naval aircraft and the defenses against attack by aircraft both at sea and on land is included.

There is also a look into the future to see what technological developments in combat aircraft we can expect to see before the end of the century. Finally, there is a short history of the ways in which aircraft have been used in war, a glossary of the more common aviation terms, and a list of the different types of combat aircraft in the service of the air forces of over twenty of the world's major military powers.

Contents

Above: Boeing B-52 Stratofortress crew scramble

Apart from transport aircraft, which are usually unarmed, a combat aircraft is made up of the weapons platform (which is the aircraft itself) and the weapons system (which is carried by the aircraft). In this section we are looking at the weapons platform. Any aircraft consists of the fuselage, wings and tailplane.

The things that try to stop an aircraft flying are its weight (which is counteracted by "lift" from the wings) and drag (air resistance), which is counteracted by the thrust of its engines. In order to reduce the drag, the designer tries to make the fuselage as streamlined as possible, to give it a good aerodynamic shape. He is, however, limited in this by the equipment that must be contained inside the fuselage. First, there must be enough room for the crew, and for the engines. A great deal of space in a modern aircraft is also taken up with the avionics – the many electronic systems that enable the aircraft to fly and carry out its role. A study of the cutaway drawing of the Air Defense Version of the Panavia Tornado shows just how much space is taken up with avionics.

The wings

An aircraft's wings give it lift. The wing is specially shaped so that the air flowing over the top of it does so faster than that underneath. This results in greater air pressure below than above, and it is this pressure which provides lift by "pushing" the wing upward. The further the wings are swept back, the less drag there is, and the faster the aircraft can fly. In order to get the best possible performance at all speeds, "swing-wing", or variable geometry aircraft have been developed, of which Tornado is a good example. Here the "sweep" of the wings can be altered by the pilot to match his speed requirements.

Control surfaces

In order to maneuver the aircraft in flight, there are control surfaces on the wings and tail. On the rear edges of the wings are ailerons, adjustment of which causes the aircraft to roll. The rudder at the rear of the tail acts like that on a boat, controlling the yaw (or left to right movement), while the elevators on the horizontal tailplanes cause the aircraft to pitch – to dive or climb. The pilot uses his control column and foot pedals to operate these. The control surfaces are linked to the cockpit controls by hydraulics, or by electronic systems called fly-by-wire.

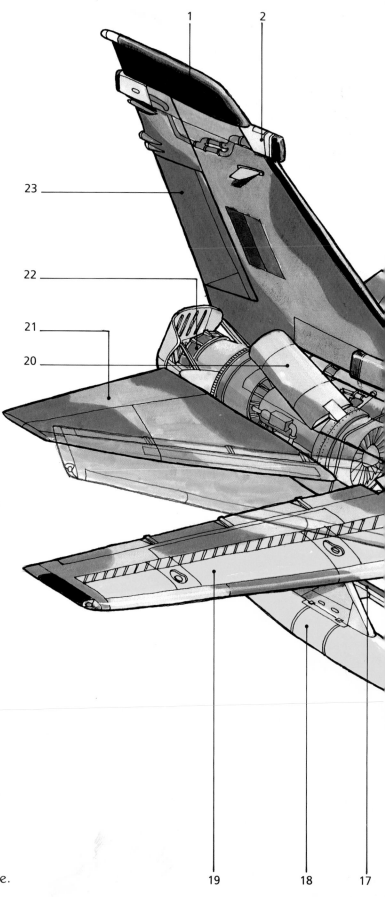

Panavia Tornado F Mk 2 Air Defence Version

This aircraft is a variant of the Tornado Multi-role Combat Aircraft, which has been developed jointly by the British, Germans and Italians. It is a two-seater with pilot and navigator, and this particular version has been designed for the RAF as an interceptor fighter to defend British air space. The wings are shown in their normal subsonic configuration, which is at an angle of 68° to the fuselage, but they can be swept back to an angle of 25° when the aircraft goes supersonic. It is armed with a 27mm cannon, and Sidewinder and Skyflash air-to-air missiles. Four Skyflash can be carried under the fuselage, with one Sidewinder under each wing. In front of the pilot is a radar for locating enemy aircraft.

Combat range

The engine intakes are on either side of the fuselage to the rear of the navigator, and the internal fuel tank is just forward of the engines. This tank enables the aircraft to fly 700km (435 miles), fight a ten-minute aerial combat, and have enough fuel to get back to its base. Using the external fuel tanks fitted under the wings, it can fly more than 2700km (1680 miles) in a single hop. It has a top speed of 2333 km/hr (1450 miles/hr), and needs an 800m (2625ft) runway to take off, but can land, reversing the thrust of its engines to slow it down, in 400m (1310ft). Apart from the ailerons which are made of carbon-fiber reinforced plastics, the aircraft skin is constructed of aluminum alloys. Much of its frame is made from a light but strong metal called titanium.

1 Tailfin
2 Electronic countermeasure aerials
3 Variable geometry wings
4 Fuel tank
5 Navigator's cockpit
6 Flight display and controls
7 Martin Baker ejector seats
8 Pilot's cockpit
9 Head-up display
10 Retractable refueling probe
11 Terrain-following and attack radar
12 Twin nosewheel
13 27mm Mauser cannon
14 Skyflash missiles
15 Air intakes
16 Starboard undercarriage
17 Sidewinder missile
18 External reserve fuel tank
19 Wing fuel tank
20 Air brake
21 Aileron
22 Engines
23 Rudder

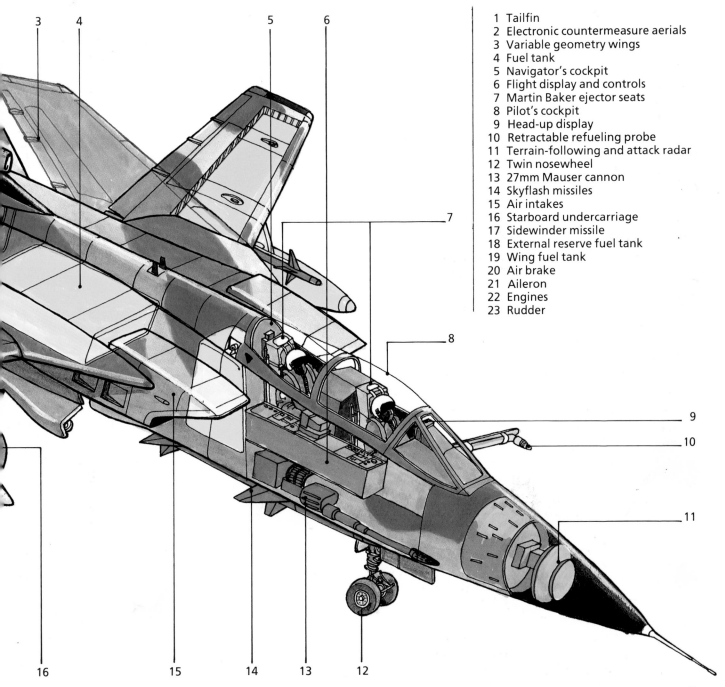

Multi-role or Special Purpose?

The modern combat aircraft has a number of roles to perform, both in fighting against other aircraft so as to achieve air superiority, and in support of ground and naval forces. The former has as its aim the defeat or suppression of the enemy's air force. This can be achieved by destroying his aircraft in the air, and is done by air superiority and interceptor aircraft. Alternatively, enemy aircraft can be destroyed on the ground on their own airfields, a task best suited to a ground attack aircraft. Support of ground and naval forces also can take various forms. Close air support means attacking the enemy on the battlefield, whether it is tanks on land or

To have a particular aircraft for each role, however, is becoming very expensive. It means that fewer aircraft of each type are bought, and therefore fewer will be made. The fewer that are built, the more expensive each individual aircraft is. Furthermore, different maintenance facilities are required by each type and pilots will need more training to fly different aircraft in different missions. More importantly, because an aircraft which can only do one job is inflexible, there may not be enough specialized aircraft available to do one particular job. Therefore, aircraft like the Tornado must be very versatile indeed.

Northrop F-20 Tigershark, a multi-role fighter

ships at sea, while "interdiction" means striking deeper into enemy territory to interrupt the flow of reinforcements and supplies. There are also two types of reconnaissance: armed reconnaissance, where an aircraft attacks targets as they pop up; and tactical reconnaissance. This means using aircraft equipped with surveillance aids like cameras to find out information about the enemy without actually attacking him.

The one for the job
Each of these jobs really needs a different type of aircraft, with differing weapons systems, radar and aircraft performance. Thus an air superiority fighter will require air-to-air missiles and be able to climb very quickly and fly very fast. A ground attack aircraft does not need the same speed or rate of climb because, if it flies too fast, it will not be able to pick up its target on the ground. While most aircraft are not protected with armor, many ground targets are, and weapons with a different type of warhead are needed to knock them out.

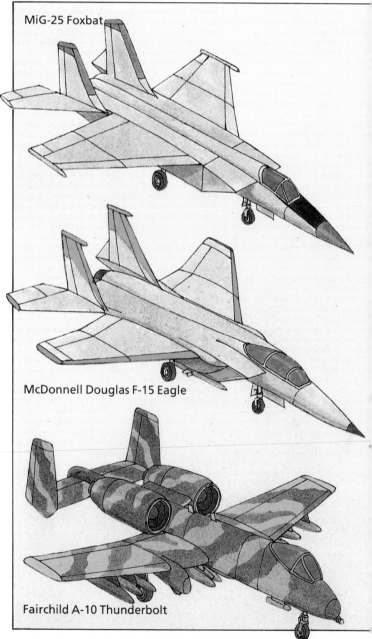

MiG-25 Foxbat

McDonnell Douglas F-15 Eagle

Fairchild A-10 Thunderbolt

Versatility

There are two solutions to this problem. The first is to design a multi-role aircraft, which can carry out a variety of tasks. The first two aircraft designed specifically for multi-role combat are the Tornado and the Swedish Viggen, although other fighters have already been adapted to carry out reconnaissance and ground attack as well as anti-aircraft missions. In the case of Tornado, its variable geometry helps give it the required performance at both high altitude for its "counter-air" role, and at low level, as a ground attack aircraft. It can also carry a wide variety of weapons.

The danger of a multi-role aircraft is that it can never do a particular job as well as an aircraft specifically designed for the task. Thus, the Tornado has a fair performance as a fighter, but in a close-in dogfight with a US F-15 or F-16, it would not win.

On the other hand, neither of the latter can remain in the air as long, having very much shorter "loiter times" – the ability to hang around and wait for trouble to develop.

A cheaper solution is to create a family of aircraft using as many of the same parts as possible, but with variants designed for a specific task. A good example is the Tornado Air Defense variant. This is slightly longer in the fuselage than the basic Tornado, in order to fit in the four Skyflash missiles. It also has different avionics systems and a sleeker nose, incorporating a different radar.

To understand the problem of different tasks better, shown below are various types of missions, and how they would be flown by three specialized aircraft: the Russian MiG-25 Foxbat (an interceptor), the US F-15 Eagle (an air superiority fighter), and the US A-10 Thunderbolt (a ground attack aircraft).

Interceptor (Hi Hi Hi)
MiG-25 Foxbat

The main task of an interceptor fighter is to tackle incoming bombers which will be flying at high altitude. Here the Soviet Foxbat takes off and climbs as steeply as possible to gain height quickly. It engages two bombers, and returns at high altitude. This is called a Hi Hi Hi profile.

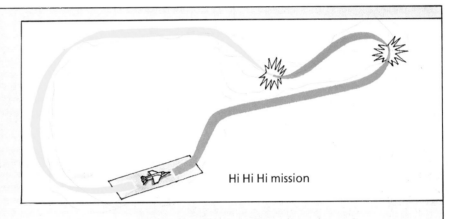

Hi Hi Hi mission

Air superiority (Hi Lo Hi)
F-15 Eagle

The US F-15 climbs quickly, but spots a ground attack aircraft at low level, and dives to attack. Designed to give its best performance at high level, it quickly regains height before returning to its base. It has used a Hi Lo Hi profile.

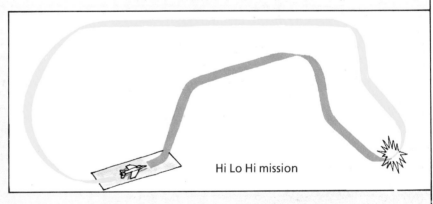

Hi Lo Hi mission

Interdiction (Lo Lo Lo)
A-10 Thunderbolt

A ground attack aircraft usually flies very low in order to avoid air superiority fighters, evade ground defenses and then identify its targets. The A-10 has here attacked two predesignated targets, and has then looked for another in order to use up its ammunition.

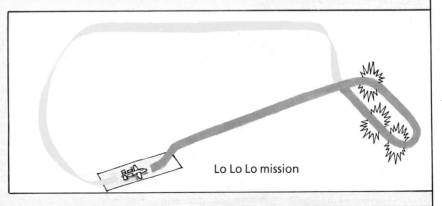

Lo Lo Lo mission

The Jet Engine

The aircraft engine produces the necessary thrust to counteract drag; drag increases with speed so, to allow really high speeds, the engine's thrust must increase by more than the drag does. Until 1945, almost all combat aircraft had piston-driven engines which operated propellers. The propeller gives an aircraft its forward speed by accelerating the flow of air past it, pulling the aircraft through the air. There is, however, a maximum speed at which the propeller can turn. Furthermore at high altitudes there is less air to work on, and hence the propeller becomes inefficient. So propeller-driven aircraft can operate only at a limited height and speed.

Early jets

In order to overcome these limitations, Sir Frank Whittle took out a patent in Britain in 1930 for a jet engine. The Germans, too, were pursuing the same line, and their Heinkel He 178 was the first jet aircraft to fly, in August 1939. This was followed by the British Gloster Whittle in 1941. The first jet to be used in combat was the Gloster Meteor at the end of July 1944, followed very quickly by the German Me 262. These early jets could not be caught easily by propeller-driven fighters, but their high fuel consumption meant that they could not stay airborne for very long and so were therefore not as an effective a threat in the air as they might well have been.

In the years since 1945 almost all combat aircraft have gone over to jet engines. Ever more efficient jet systems have been introduced to enable aircraft to fly higher and faster and to remain in the air for longer periods of operational duty.

Dassault Breguet Super Mirage 4000: a typical turbofan

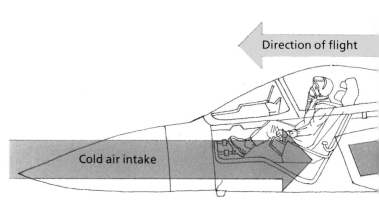

Direction of flight

Cold air intake

How a jet engine works

The jet engine is comparatively simple. As the aircraft flies, cold air is drawn into the engine through its intakes. The air is fed into a compressor and compressed, and then passes to the engine itself. Here, fuel is burned and combines with the compressed air to produce extremely hot gases. These expand inside the

Turbofan

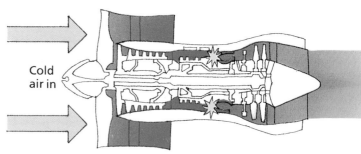

Cold air in

Vectored thrust

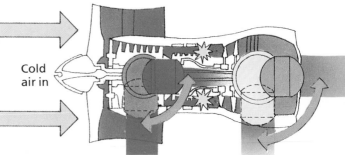

Cold air in

Turbofan and vectored thrust

In order to produce greater thrust the compressor has fan-like blades which draw in more air than the turbojet. Some of this air passes directly into the engine. The remainder bypasses the engine and joins the hot exhaust gases, giving them greater mass and thrust. A turbofan variant is the vectored thrust engine used on the Harrier. By altering the direction of the thrust, the Harrier can take off and land vertically.

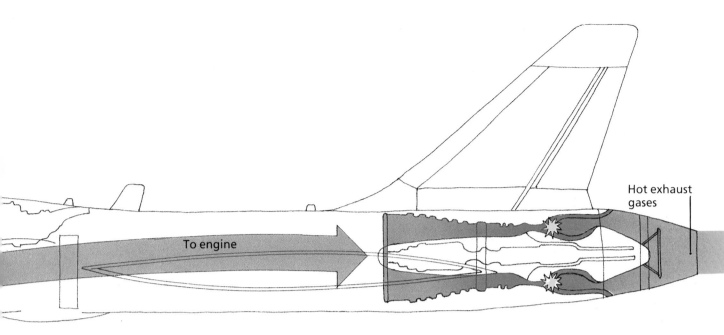

To engine

Hot exhaust gases

engine then leave at very high speed via an exhaust pipe; the thrust is given to the aircraft by the force of the exhaust gases pushing the engine forward. The greater the mass of the exhaust gases and their acceleration, the more thrust is produced. On its way out the gas drives a turbine which powers the compressor. There are, however, different types of jet engines.

Turbojet

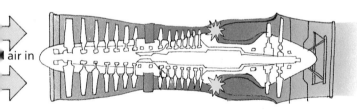

air in

Turboprop

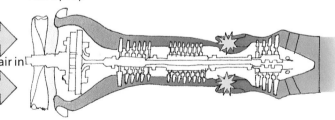

air in

Turbojet and turboprop
The basic jet engine described above is called a turbojet. The fastest US airplane, the SR-71, is powered by the turbojet. It is used for trainers, ground attack aircraft and some transports. The turboprop differs from the turbojet in that the turbine also drives a propeller, as on a piston-engined aircraft. This is more economical on fuel, and is used on aircraft which do not need high speeds, but have to stay airborne a long time.

Other jet variants
Another way of improving the performance of the jet engine is the use of reheat, or after-burners. Here the hot gases are reignited after they leave the engine, producing greater acceleration, and hence greater thrust. More fuel is needed, and the pilots of high-performance fighters tend to use after-burners just for gaining height quickly (when taking off, for example) and will shut them off for normal flying. The ultimate in supersonic flight is the ramjet, which is the simplest form of jet engine. The forward motion of the engine literally "rams" the air in, and no compressor is needed. However, it cannot operate below speeds of Mach 2 (twice the speed of sound), so an aircraft would need a rocket-assisted takeoff to reach this speed.

High speed jets land at very high speeds and often need braking parachutes to slow them down. Another method is to put the engines into reverse thrust, and this is used by some combat aircraft and by commercial airliners.

Grumman E2C Hawkeye: a typical turboprop

Flight Crew

The modern combat aircraft represents some of the most advanced technology in the world today. This is particularly true of the electronics used in today's aircraft. These automatically navigate the aircraft at supersonic speed to a point hundreds of miles away and help attack and destroy high-speed targets, often without the pilot even seeing the target. Yet, in spite of all the "magic black boxes" which the aircraft has, the ultimate control rests in the hands of human beings. However sophisticated the aircraft is, it can only be as good as the crew which fly it.

Apart from transport and big surveillance aircraft, which need larger crews because they are airborne for long periods of time, most combat aircraft are single or two-seaters. Ideally, the former is preferred by aircraft designers, as it enables them to keep the aircraft more compact. But often there are too many functions for one man to carry out, and a navigator is brought in to help the pilot out.

Crew tasks

Many of the tasks outlined here will be examined in greater detail in the following pages, but taken together they give a good idea of how demanding it can be to fly a modern aircraft. Obviously, the most important task is actually flying the aircraft – to handle a supersonic fighter takes quick thinking and speed of reaction, and perfect coordination between brain, hands and feet. Navigation is the next most important job. The pilot must know exactly where he is at any moment, and be able to get the aircraft to the right place at the right time. If he is engaging a target, he must decide on the most effective weapon to use against it, and launch it at the right moment to score a "hit." He must also constantly monitor his instruments to ensure that all systems are operating

correctly. There are radios to operate and radars to monitor. Finally, electronic warfare plays a large part in modern air warfare. Aircraft carry a number of offensive and defensive electronic devices, and these must be monitored and operated.

Crew training

To train a fast-jet pilot properly takes about three years. He will first of all attend a selection board to establish that he has the intelligence and natural aptitude for flying. He will learn to fly on a basic trainer with a piston engine and then on a very simple jet. From his performance on the jet he is selected for multi-engine, fast-jet or helicopter advanced training. The fast-jet pilot will do this on an advanced jet trainer, like the Northrop T-38, with all the characteristics of a combat aircraft and which often, like the British Aerospace Hawk, has an important combat role in times of war. Once he has passed through this, he will then be trained on the frontline aircraft he has been selected to fly. Much use is made of advanced computer-controlled flight simulators, which save flying hours and the risk of losing aircraft and pilot in an accident. The pilot also spends long hours learning everything about the aircraft he is to fly – the more he understands his machine, the better he will handle it. Navigators also undergo long training, and once fully trained, both navigator and pilot spend long hours practicing, both in the air and on the ground, to perfect their skills.

The ejector seat

The crew's lifesaver in a high-speed jet, where everything happens so quickly, is the ejector seat. This enables them to "bail out" of the aircraft quickly and safely if something goes wrong. The diagram below shows how it works.

Ejector seat
1 Pilot presses button which ignites rockets attached to seat and blows off cockpit hood. 2 Pilot and seat are blasted clear of aircraft. 3 Mini chute fills with air and begins to draw out main parachute. 4 Main parachute begins to fill with air. 5 Main chute is filled and pilot floats gently to earth.

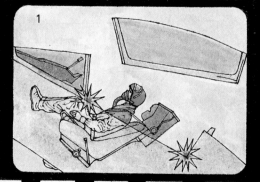

Route planning

Before any mission is flown, the route the aircraft is to take must be carefully planned. In the old days this meant working out courses and bearings, and often using mental arithmetic to work out when the aircraft's heading should be changed. Nowadays, the on-board computer makes all this very much easier, and is essential equipment in a high-speed jet. First, the pilot works out his flight plan and feeds it into a computer (in a two seat jet this is the navigator's job). The plan will include prominent landmarks, areas to be avoided, target locations and spare reference points in case the plan is changed during the flight. The course is then displayed as a dotted line on a radar map, with the aircraft shown as a circle. The pilot merely has to keep the circle on the dotted line.

The flying suit

Having the right type of flying clothing is very important. Here is a pilot in a typical helmet and flying suit. His helmet is like a motorcyclist's crash helmet, complete with anti-glare visor. It also incorporates headphones to enable him to listen to his radio and his navigator, if he has one. Around his neck he wears a lifejacket. He also has a mouthpiece: this is primarily an oxygen mask, but it includes a microphone for his radio. His flying suit is one-piece and made of flame resistant material. Under it he will wear a "G" or high pressure suit to enable his body to stand up to the pressures of high-speed flight. He also has other pockets by his ankles, and a knife to enable him to cut himself free if he is trapped. Both the oxygen tube and radio cable connect up to sockets in the cockpit.

Pilot in full flying suit

Ground route planning

Navigator feeding in route plan to on-board computer

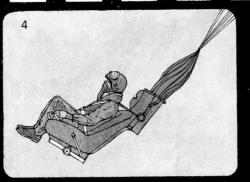

The Hot Seat

To the outsider, the cockpit of a combat aircraft is completely bewildering. The number of knobs, switches and dials make one wonder how the pilot can ever find his way around them. To him, however, they are little more complicated than those in a car, and many of them fulfill the same functions. To begin with, the pilot needs the controls for actually flying the aircraft, and he also needs instruments to tell him how fast he is going, how much fuel he has left and what temperature his engines are at – no different from a car. He also needs to know quickly if there is something wrong with the aircraft, so he has a series of warning lights.

Flying instruments

He also has another series of instruments called the "head down" display. These enable him to fly the aircraft using instruments alone, which he will often do at high altitude, in darkness or in conditions of poor visibility. The most important of these is the artificial horizon. If a pilot cannot see the horizon, it is very easy for him to lose his sense of direction. This instrument therefore gives him an artificial horizon to use as a reference point. He may also

Rockwell B1-B Operator's station

have a "head up" display, as described opposite.

Next there are the various navigation systems, which we have already discussed. Then there are the radios, and the pilot needs controls to operate these. He also has consoles for his weapons systems, enabling him to select and fire the right weapon for each target.

Boeing B-52 Stratofortress flight deck and crew

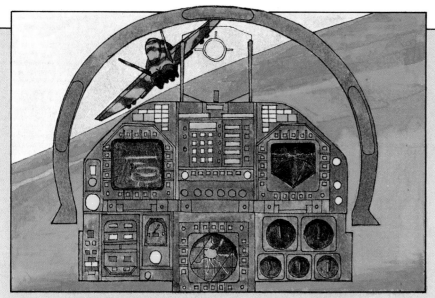

General Dynamics F-16 Head Up Display

The HUD

The Head Up Display (HUD) is the modern version of a weapons sight, but it is very much more than just a sight. Besides enabling the pilot to take the correct aim in order to hit his target, it also gives him flight instrument and navigational information so that he does not have to look down at his cockpit instruments while making his attack. The HUD is designed so that the pilot needn't refocus his eyes to read the display: every second counts in high-speed combat.

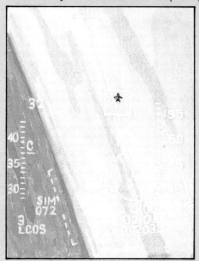

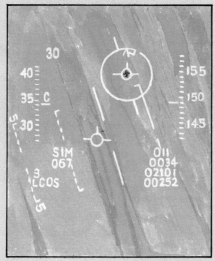

Target engagement

Here is what the HUD on the US F-16 fighter looks like. The left hand picture shows the target inside a square box, which indicates that the radar has locked onto it. The vertical scales on either side give the aircraft's speed and height. The big circle is the weapons sight itself. The radar and computers give details of the target's flight path, and the pilot uses these to line the sight up with the target. The second picture shows that he has done this.

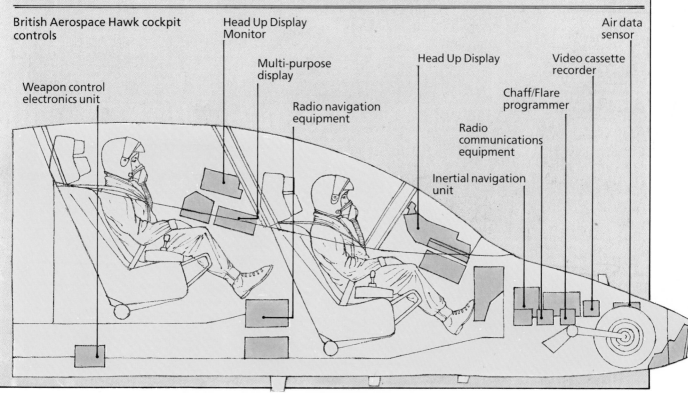

British Aerospace Hawk cockpit controls

Head Up Display Monitor

Multi-purpose display

Radio navigation equipment

Weapon control electronics unit

Head Up Display

Air data sensor

Video cassette recorder

Chaff/Flare programmer

Radio communications equipment

Inertial navigation unit

Weapons Systems

There is a wide variety of airborne weapon systems available. They can be classified into two main types: air-to-air for attacking other aircraft; and air-to-ground.

Air-to-air weapons appear in the form of missiles and cannon. The former are divided into short, medium and long range systems. The US Hughes Phoenix has the longest range of any – over 200km (124 miles) – and is radar-guided. Medium range missiles have ranges of between 15km and 60km (9-37 miles), and usually use what is called semi-active radar homing guidance. The attacking aircraft sends radar signals, which reflect off the target and are picked up by the missile, which homes in on them. Good examples of this are the British Skyflash and US Sparrow. Short range missiles like the US Sidewinder, on the other hand, tend to be "fire and forget" systems, which means that, once launched, the pilot does not have to guide them onto the target. They usually pick up the infrared radiation produced by the heat of the exhaust gases of the target and lock onto this. A target aircraft usually tries to avoid them by launching decoy heat sources in the form of flares, and hopes that the missile will be distracted by these. Cannon are used only when very close to the target, and are normally 20-30mm in caliber.

Ground attack

There are many different air-to-surface weapons. These use different forms of guidance, including infrared, television, laser and antiradiation. The last pick up radar signals and fly straight toward the radar aerial, destroying it and "blinding" the defenses. Lasers are becoming very popular as a means of guidance. Television and laser are also used with what are called "smart" bombs. These guide the weapon to its target with extraordinary accuracy, and can be launched when the aircraft is some way from the target. Nevertheless, "dumb" or traditional "iron" bombs are still widely used in weights ranging from 115-900kg (250-2000lbs). These can be filled with high explosive or napalm.

Rockets

Unguided rockets are also widely used. They are usually around 60mm in caliber and are mounted in pods, with up to thirty rockets in each pod. Cluster bomb units are very popular as "area weapons." These consist of a large number of "bomblets" which spread out over a strip of land 250 yards long and 100 yards wide and are usually used against armor and infantry. Two other types of weapon which are described in more detail opposite are used to attack airfields.

Rearmed Panavia Tornado GR1 on takeoff

Combat ready

With such a wide range of weapons available, it is possible to fit a variety to a combat aircraft depending on its mission. Opposite is a table showing possible variations. The only fixed weapons on the aircraft shown are its cannon, and everything else is attached under its fuselage or wings. Each fixing point or pylon has a maximum weight and this and the weapon shape dictates what can be fitted to it. The weapons load must also be balanced so as not to upset the flying trim of the aircraft, and there is a maximum weapons weight which it can carry. Thus, once the aircraft's mission is known, it is a question of juggling the weapons load in order to carry out the mission in the most effective way. If it is to be at long range, then external fuel tanks may have to be carried under the wings which will mean fewer weapons can be fitted.

Runway penetration

When attacking airfields, the two main targets are runways and aircraft on the ground. The latter are usually kept in specially hardened shelters while runways are hardened as well, so special weapons are used. These have penetrators to pierce the concrete before the warhead explodes, and this will dig craters in the runway or destroy the aircraft in their shelters. These projectiles often have parachutes to ensure that the penetrator strikes at the right angle.

Modular bomb

This is a new idea for a submunition weapon. Two or three explosive modules are contained in one cylindrical bomb. When the aircraft releases the bomb, a drogue parachute draws out each module, which then floats to earth on a main parachute. The modules can be set to explode in the air or on the ground, and will shower the immediate area with metal fragments which can penetrate thin armor plate.

Dassault Breguet
Mirage 2000

Typical weapon loads

	300kg (660lbs)	1800kg (4000lbs)	400kg (880lbs)	400kg (880lbs)	1800kg (4000lbs)	400kg (880lbs)	400kg (880lbs)	1800kg (4000lbs)	300kg (660lbs)
Air-to-air missiles		●			●			●	
Close-combat missiles	●	●						●	●
250kg (550lbs) bombs	●	●●●●	●	●	●●●●	●	●	●●●●	●
1000kg (2200lbs) bombs		●			●			●	
68mm (2½in) rocket launchers	●	●						●	
100mm (4in) rocket launchers		●						●	
Reserve fuel tanks		●			●			●	
Runway penetration bombs	●	●●●	●	●	●●●	●	●	●●●	●
Modular bombs		●	●	●	●	●	●		
Combined stores adaptors		●						●	
Gun pods				●		●			
Reconnaissance pods					●				
250kg (550lbs) bombs			●	●	●●	●	●		
Air-to-surface missiles		●			●			●	
Weapons guidance pods				●					

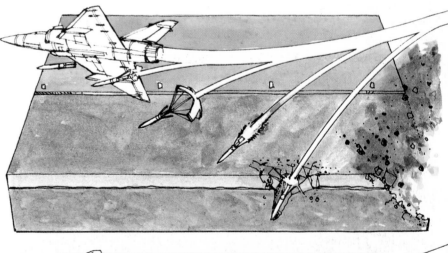

17

The Electronics Duel

Electronics systems play a vital role in air warfare. The modern combat aircraft is very dependent on them for navigation, reconnaissance, and acquiring and engaging targets. Probably the most important are the aircraft's radars and those on the ground.

In terms of navigation, radar is very important when flying at low level. Here terrain-following forward-looking radar is used. The radar in the nose of the aircraft sends out signals which are reflected by the terrain, and a TV-type display gives the pilot the shape of the countryside over which he is about to fly, enabling him to avoid hills. In the more sophisticated systems, the radar is linked to the autopilot and the aircraft's computers. The aircraft then flies automatically. Normally, terrain-following radars are preset to a particular altitude. The aircraft will fly at this height with the radar only picking out ground features above it. Downward looking radar is also tied in to the radar map display.

Radar

In order to pick up targets in the air, whether it is an enemy aircraft or a friendly refueling tanker, the pilot will instruct the radar to search in a particular direction and range band. When the radar has spotted the target (that is, when it receives a reflected signal) it will lock onto it, and this enables the pilot to close with it. If it is an enemy aircraft, he might well use a radar-guided missile to destroy it. The enemy will do his best to jam these radars, and this is known as Electronic Counter Measures

(ECM). In order to protect against this, Electronic Counter Counter Measures (ECCM) will be used.

Friend or foe?

All combat aircraft carry a piece of equipment called an Identification Friend or Foe (IFF) device. This sends out a signal which will receive an automatic response from a friendly aircraft. With combat aircraft flying at high speed, this is often the only way that a pilot can tell if an aircraft is hostile; if the enemy can jam or "fool" an IFF system, he is going to be in difficulties. The normal method of jamming is to send out signals on the enemy's radar frequency, this will blot out his display or fool it by giving the enemy's IFF signal. Another method, which is used to deflect radar guided missiles, is to release "chaff," strips of metal which will reflect radar signals and confuse the radar. Aircraft also carry radar warning devices which tell the pilot when a radar has locked onto him. If he finds that an infrared-homing missile is on his tail, then he can drop a "flare" – a piece of very hot, burning magnesium on a parachute which attracts the missile away from the aircraft.

Because electronic warfare devices are so vital in modern air combat, their details are kept very secret so that a potential enemy cannot develop counter-measures against them. Much effort also goes into designing radars and communications equipment which are as well protected as possible against interference from enemy electronic counter measures.

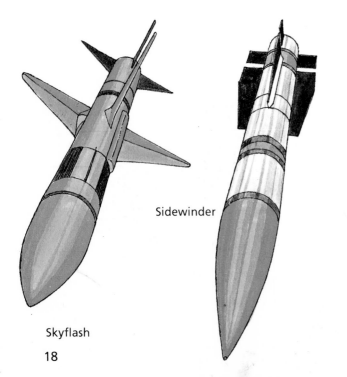

Sidewinder

Skyflash

Phoenix

Missile systems
Skyflash, Sidewinder and Phoenix are three of the most deadly air-to-air missiles in use today. Skyflash has a greater range than Sidewinder, which is designed for high acceleration to attack fast-moving targets. Phoenix was developed for use exclusively from the F-14 Tomcat. The F-14's maximum load of six Phoenix can be fired almost simultaneously to engage separate targets. Shown opposite are the Raytheon cluster bomb used against ground forces and the Wallop Masquerade which releases chaff to "fool" enemy radars.

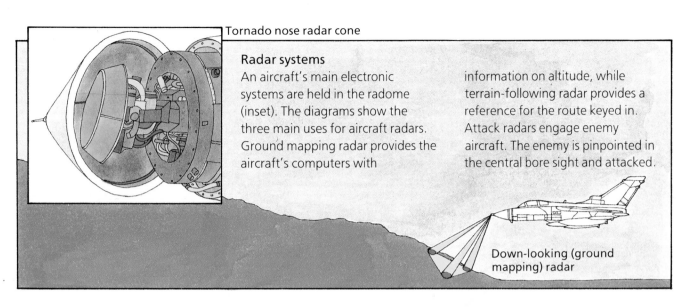

Tornado nose radar cone

Radar systems

An aircraft's main electronic systems are held in the radome (inset). The diagrams show the three main uses for aircraft radars. Ground mapping radar provides the aircraft's computers with information on altitude, while terrain-following radar provides a reference for the route keyed in. Attack radars engage enemy aircraft. The enemy is pinpointed in the central bore sight and attacked.

Down-looking (ground mapping) radar

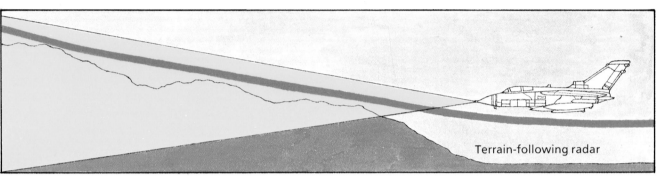

Terrain-following radar

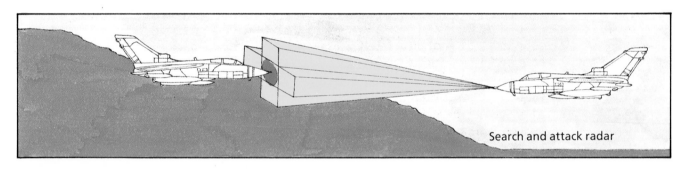

Search and attack radar

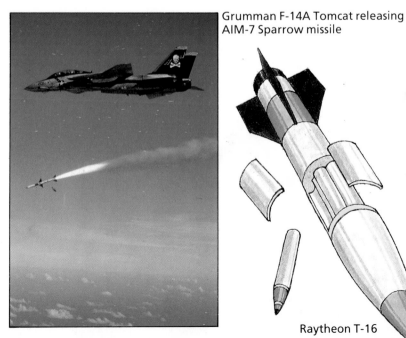

Grumman F-14A Tomcat releasing AIM-7 Sparrow missile

Raytheon T-16

Wallop Masquerade

Strategic Bombers

While offensive air support and interdiction aircraft give direct or indirect support to the land or sea battle, strategic bombers are designed to strike deep into the enemy's country. In the years after World War 1 many airmen believed that bombers on their own could win wars by attacking centers of industry and the civilian morale, but it was proved in World War 2 that this could not be done. However, when nuclear weapons were invented and then used to force Japan to surrender in 1945, the strategic bomber gained a new lease of life. Although it can still be used with conventional weapons, its normal role nowadays is as a nuclear bomber, as a member of what the Americans call the nuclear triad, along with land-based and submarine-launched nuclear missiles. Both the Americans and the Russians possess strategic bombers and we will look at some of the types in service and how they are used.

Rockwell B-1B

This is the latest of the US strategic bombers, and is expected to enter service in 1986. Powered by four reheat turbofan engines, it has variable geometry wings. Top speed is Mach 1.5, normal cruising speed is about 850km/h (530 mph). It also flies at high speed at very low altitudes. On its internal fuel tanks it has a range of some 12,000km (7460 miles), and a crew of four – two pilots and two systems operators, who take care of the navigation, weapons and electronic warfare systems. It can carry a weapons load of some 40,000kg (88,180lbs). This can include conventional or nuclear iron bombs, and two types of nuclear missile. The first is the Short Range Attack Missile, which flies supersonically at treetop height and can be launched 160km (100 miles) from target. This, however, is being largely replaced by the Air-Launched Cruise Missile.

Cruise missile

The Air-Launched Cruise Missile is similar to the ground-launched version, now being deployed in Europe by NATO. Its effectiveness lies in its ability to fly at very low level, and this with its small size makes it very difficult to detect. It has a range of 2400km (1490 miles), which means that the aircraft can launch it from well inside safe friendly territory.

It is very accurate, which makes it ideal for knocking out small targets like nuclear missile launchers. Its route to the target is preplanned and

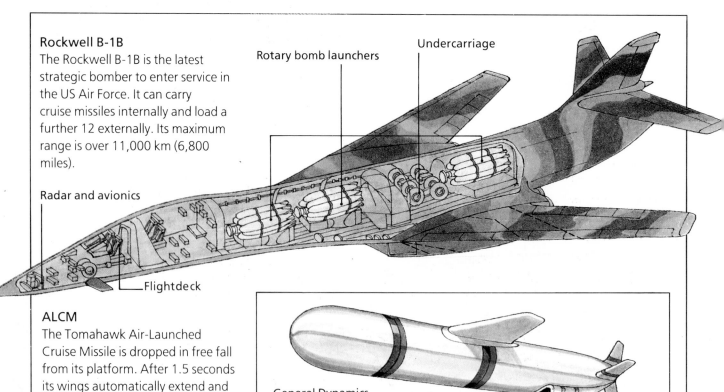

Rockwell B-1B
The Rockwell B-1B is the latest strategic bomber to enter service in the US Air Force. It can carry cruise missiles internally and load a further 12 externally. Its maximum range is over 11,000 km (6,800 miles).

Radar and avionics

Rotary bomb launchers

Undercarriage

Flightdeck

ALCM
The Tomahawk Air-Launched Cruise Missile is dropped in free fall from its platform. After 1.5 seconds its wings automatically extend and the turbofan engine fires. Note the air intake at the rear.

General Dynamics
Tomahawk Air-Launched Cruise Missile

Tupolev TU-16 Badger

Tupolev TU-20 Bear and USAF F-4 Phantom chase planes

General Dynamics F-111

Tomahawk II Medium Range Air-to-surface missile loading on to B-52D Stratofortress

stored in the missile's computer and this, in combination with a radar altimeter, keeps the missile on course. Once it gets near the target, it switches on another guidance system. This uses radar, optical and infrared sensors to produce a picture of the target, which is then compared with a picture stored in the computer. The computer then steers the missile on a course that will make the two pictures match up. Such is its accuracy that, after a flight of 2400km (1490 miles) it can guarantee to strike within 50m (164ft) of the target. Its only drawback is its low speed.

Other strategic bomber types

One of the most well-known bombers is the Boeing B-52, which has been flying for over thirty years. Similar to the B-1B, it can be used at low level, although originally designed for high altitude flying. It has a radius of action of just under 6000km (3730 miles). It carries the same weapons as the B-1B, but has a relic of the World War 2 bomber in that it has a remotely operated machine gun or automatic cannon turret in the tail. The B-52's greatest claim to fame was in Vietnam, when incredibly heavy bombing of jungle areas literally altered the map. The Russians, too, have large bombers, the Bear and the Bison. The Bear is the largest turboprop aircraft to achieve a front line role, and has a maximum range of 12,550km (7800 miles). The Bison was the first long range strategic jet bomber, contemporary to the B-52, and it can operate at a range of 11,250km (7000 miles). All the Soviet types are used for reconnaissance and maritime strike as well, and often operate over the North Sea, probing NATO air defenses.

Smaller strategic bombers

A number of smaller aircraft are also designed to be conventional and nuclear strategic bombers, although they are often used for interdiction as well. Examples of these are the Tornado, the French Mirage IVA, the American F-111 and the Russian Badger, Blinder and Backfire. They were all designed in the Sixties when it was believed that radar defenses made the high altitude bomber very vulnerable. Instead, these aircraft fly fast and low in order to get under the enemy radar. However, without air-to-air refueling, their range is limited to under 1500km (930 miles), and they carry fewer and smaller warheads than the larger type of strategic bomber. Nevertheless, they represent another nuclear delivery means, and their suitability as conventional interdiction aircraft also makes them useful for attacking enemy reinforcements and headquarters with conventional weapons like bombs and cannon.

The Battle for Intelligence

Another very important role for the combat aircraft is that of reconnaissance and intelligence gathering. This, of course, was the aircraft's original role in World War I, although it has now been joined by other aerial platforms. At the highest altitudes are the intelligence gathering satellites, or Intelsats, which constantly circle the globe, transmitting pictures back to earth. It might be thought that with sufficient numbers of them in orbit, no other means of gathering is needed, but satellites are not foolproof, and other systems are required to back them up.

Spy planes

At the next level comes the high altitude aircraft, the so-called "spy plane." The Americans have used these for a number of years, and the latest type in service, the Lockheed SR-71 Blackbird, is described opposite. They fly very fast and operate at heights of around 25,000m (82,000ft), and are very difficult to catch. They carry conventional cameras, infrared cameras for taking photographs through clouds and radar.

The next type is the Airborne Early Warning aircraft. These are very recognizable from the large saucer-shaped radar scanner carried on top of the fuselage. The scanner rotates slowly in flight and, with the aircraft flying high enough, can spot enemy aircraft over 300km (186 miles) away. It is particularly useful for picking up aircraft flying at low level. It can also be used as an airborne command post to coordinate the movement of friendly aircraft and direct their operations.

Aircraft are also still used for tactical reconnaissance, which produces intelligence that will effect the immediate land battle. Much of it is directed to locating the enemy's reinforcements and other targets which can then be attacked by interdiction aircraft or long-range artillery and ground-based missiles. Sideways Looking Airborne Radar normally takes the form of a thin oblong box mounted below the fuselage, and literally looks sideways. Its main advantage is that the aircraft can fly up and down in friendly territory and watch what the enemy is doing without flying over them.

Lockheed SR-71

Boeing E-3A Sentry AWAC

Lockheed TR-1

Lockheed SR-71 Blackbird

This has been in service with the US Air Force since about 1965. The aircraft holds the world air speed record, Mach 3.31, and normally operates at 25,000m (82,000ft). Although it can loiter at lower speeds for up to seven hours, at maximum speed it can only fly for 90 minutes without refueling. Its special camera can, however, cover 200km (125 miles) at one shot and its quality is such that a golf ball can be detected from 16km (10 miles).

Reconnaissance

An increasingly popular type of reconnaissance aircraft is the Remotely Piloted Vehicle (RPV). This is a small unmanned airplane controlled from the ground like a radio-controlled model. Remotely piloted vehicles can also be used to locate targets and mark them with laser beams for laser-guided bombs and shells.

Satellite reconnaissance

Details of satellite reconnaissance platforms are kept highly secret and the exact degree of resolution of their optical and infrared cameras are a matter for speculation, but it is known they can detect very small objects from 160km (100 miles) in space. Both Superpowers have a network of missile early warning satellites, ready to detect any launch of inter-continental ballistic missiles. Undoubtedly, satellites and reconnaissance aircraft work together to build up a picture of enemy troop exercises, shipping movements and aircraft activity.

Spy satellite and ground photographs

The Weightlifters

Military transport aircraft are not glamorous, but are nonetheless a key part of any country's air force. There are two categories of transport – strategic lift and tactical lift. The former flies troops and supplies to a theater of war, while the latter operate within that theater.

Strategic transport aircraft give a country, especially a global power like the USA or USSR, the ability to reinforce or intervene in any part of the world very quickly. Examples of this are the Soviet intervention in Afghanistan in December 1979, the American "air bridge" by which she reinforces her troops in Europe in time of tension, and her Rapid Deployment Force, which is designed to intervene if there is a threat to oil supplies in the Persian Gulf.

Smaller aircraft

Tactical transport aircraft are smaller and have a more limited range, and are often designed to take off and land on very short, makeshift runways.

Transport aircraft deliver troops and supplies in two ways. They can either land with them, or drop them by parachute. To land troops and supplies safely requires the use of an airstrip which is not under enemy fire, but the US Air Force developed a technique in Vietnam of landing an aircraft under fire, pushing supplies out while the aircraft was taxiing and then immediately taking off again. Alternatively, the aircraft can do a very low pass over the runway and the supplies can be pushed out.

Also to make loading and unloading as simple as possible, most transport aircraft are fitted with large doors in the rear of the fuselage.

Air tankers

Strategic bombers, high altitude and maritime reconnaissance aircraft and fighters are also often very reliant on air tankers. A typical tanker can fly 2415km (1500 miles) and offload 60 tonnes (59 tons) of fuel. It can refuel up to three aircraft at once, using a drogue attached to each wing, and one which is let down from the fuselage. This requires extreme skill. A recent example took place in May 1982 during the Falkland Islands War. An RAF Vulcan on a raid flew a round trip of some 12,500km (7770 miles) from Ascension Island to Port Stanley and required eleven Victor tankers during the fight.

Lockheed C-5 Galaxy

Shorts Skyvan
A typical tactical transport, which has a range of 380km (236 miles) fully loaded and a maximum speed of 320km/h (199mph).

Lockheed C-130 Hercules
This is one of the most successful military aircraft of all time. It has been flying for thirty years, and is likely still to be in service at the turn of the century. It has a normal range of 4000km (2486 miles).

Lockheed C-141 Starlifter
This was the first jet-powered military transport to come into service, and is the mainstay of the US Air Force Military Airlift Command. Fully loaded, it has a range of almost 4800km (2980 miles).

Lockheed C-5 Galaxy
This is one of the largest aircraft in the world, with a range of 5600km (3480 miles) fully loaded and almost 12,000km (7460 miles) when empty. It can carry two M-60 main battle tanks.

Boeing CH-47 Chinook
A medium-lift helicopter with a range of 160km (100 miles).

McDonnell-Douglas KC-10A Extenders during ''buddy buddy'' refueling

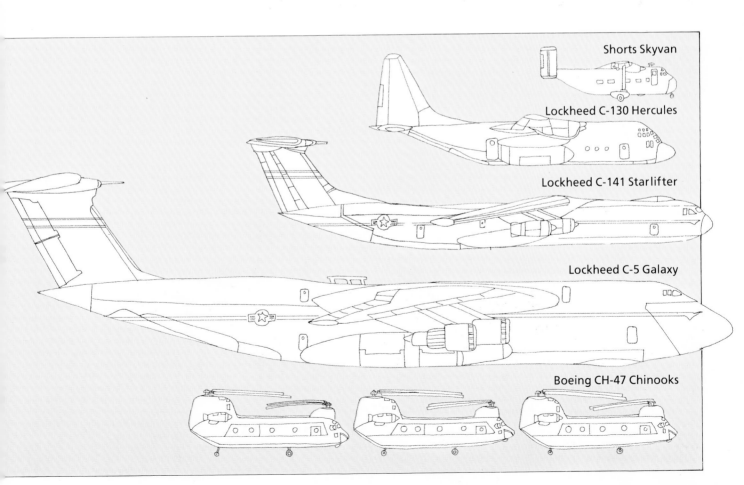

Shorts Skyvan

Lockheed C-130 Hercules

Lockheed C-141 Starlifter

Lockheed C-5 Galaxy

Boeing CH-47 Chinooks

The Airfield in Action

An airfield exists to keep aircraft flying. This involves not just the air crew, but many other people as well. First of all are the ground crews who maintain the aircraft, and their duties are described below. Then there are the air traffic controllers, who work in the control tower. It is their job to control the movement of aircraft on and above the airfield, rather like policemen on traffic duty. They use radars covering both the airfield itself and the sky overhead, and when many aircraft are landing and taking off it is a very demanding job. If the controller's attention wanders, then fatal accidents can happen.

Weather is a very important element in flying operations, and each airfield will have its own meteorologist. There are also intelligence experts, who will brief the pilots on the enemy situation and examine the information, including photographs, which they bring back. There are also people who look after the various supplies – spare parts, fuel, weapons – and those who carry out the more complicated maintenance and repair tasks. Signals and radar experts are also needed.

Hardened shelter and ground crew

In wartime aircraft are always kept in hardened shelters to protect them, and would not be left outside as in the picture below. The ground crew is preparing an aircraft for a mission. This involves fueling and arming it, and checking that everything is working. Often a ground crew will have a particular aircraft to look after, and will get to know it and its pilot well. The crew will also spend much time carrying out routine servicing and maintenance.

Airfield Air Traffic Control

Support structure

The airfield also has to be defended, and will have a number of ground-based air defense weapons. There will also be a large number of people involved in administrative tasks. Cooks, accountants, chaplains, doctors, dentists and drivers all have their parts to play. It can be seen, therefore, that it takes a large number of people to keep an aircraft flying.

Makeshift airfields

Because large airfields are very vulnerable to attack since the enemy knows where they are, aircraft will often operate from makeshift airfields. The Harrier, with its vertical takeoff and landing (VTOL) capability, is ideal for this, and will often operate from a clearing in a wood. Special matting is used on the landing pad to ensure that debris does not

Panavia Tornado GR1 and Hardened Aircraft Shelter (HAS)

Tornado ground crew in HAS

SEPECAT Jaguar taking off from motorway

get sucked up into the engines. For aircraft which need a longer takeoff, life is more difficult.

In parts of Europe, tests have been carried out which prove that a motorway makes an excellent runway. The occasional bridge over the motorway is an ideal place to hide an aircraft. Otherwise, runways can be made from strips of steel matting laid over level grass.

An operational sortie

On an airfield a number of aircraft will always be instantly ready to take off, fully armed and fueled, and often with the pilot already strapped in his cockpit. He will be briefed on his mission: this will include telling him his task as well as all the latest information about the enemy in the area in which he is to operate. This takes no more than a couple of minutes. He then tells the control tower that he is ready for takeoff and will be ordered to taxi to the runway. He is then cleared for takeoff. Once he has completed the mission, he will pass what is called an "in-flight report" by radio to the airfield, giving an outline of how successful it was. If he is flying a close air support mission, his attack will often be directed by a ground observer, using radio or a laser target designator.

Once he is back near the airfield, the air controllers will give him landing instructions. Back on the ground, he will taxi back to his hardened shelter, and let the ground crew know of any aircraft faults or any damage which has occurred. He will then be debriefed in detail, after which he will probably have a chance to rest until it is his turn to be on readiness again.

Refueling Tornado in HAS

Rearming General Dynamics F-16

Naval Air Power

It was the campaign in the Pacific Ocean in World War II that showed how air power can influence the war at sea. Indeed, it was the aircraft carrier rather than the battleship which was the most important type of ship. More ships were sunk by carrier-borne aircraft than by other ships.

Naval air power is used in four main ways. First of all, there is maritime reconnaissance. This enables the fleet to extend the range of its ship-borne radar, which, like any radar, is limited in range by the curvature of the earth's surface. Maritime reconnaissance aircraft are designed to stay airborne for long periods of time – twelve or more hours – and this can be increased by air-to-air refueling. The illustration of USS *Nimitz* below

also shows an airborne early warning aircraft, a Grumman E-2 Hawkeye, another vital form of reconnaissance which guards against air attack. Apart from locating enemy surface ships, maritime reconnaissance aircraft also play a large part in anti-submarine warfare. They can detect submarines under the water by dropping sonobuoys, which listen for the sounds made by the submarine. Once detected, the submarine can then be attacked using air-launched torpedoes or depth charges. Helicopters, too, are often used for anti-submarine operations.

Protection of the fleet against air attack is the third main role. If there is a threat of an air attack, a naval task force commander will try and keep fighters in the air all the time to provide protection. He can, however, use his Airborne Early Warning aircraft, which will give him time to get aircraft in the air before the attack arrives.

Shipping strike
As for the final role, that of strikes against enemy shipping, the Falklands campaign showed how effective aircraft are in this type of operation. The main weapon used is the anti-ship missile. In the

USS *Nimitz*
The largest type of aircraft carrier afloat, the *Nimitz* carries over 90 aircraft and helicopters. She is carrying the single seater F-14 Tomcat with its distinctive twin tail.

British Aerospace Sea Harrier

Sea Harriers prepared for flight

past, infrared or radar-seeking missiles flew at relatively high altitudes and attacked ships from above. The French Exocet, which the Argentinians used with success in the Falklands, literally skims the surface of the water and, apart from being very fast, is very difficult to pick up on ship-borne radar. It represents a serious threat to ships, as do "smart" bombs, in that it can be launched some distance from the target.

Harrier carrier

The aircraft carrier is still the main means of providing naval air power. The Sea Harrier, with its vertical takeoff capability, can also operate from a frigate or destroyer and more than demonstrated its remarkable versatility in the Falklands. On board an aircraft carrier like the *Hermes*, the Harrier uses a ski jump to take off. This saves fuel and is quicker than vertical takeoff.

Catapult launch

Most naval aircraft, unlike the Harrier, do not have a vertical takeoff capability, and carrier flight decks are not long enough for them to be able to take off under their own power. They therefore use a catapult to help them gain flying speed quickly. The aircraft is mounted on a trolley. The pilot starts the aircraft's engines and opens the throttle wide, the trolley is propelled by a rocket and when it reaches the end of its run, it disengages from the aircraft, which now flies under its own power.

Arrester hook recovery

The fast landing speeds of jet aircraft mean that they also need help to land as well as take off. The hook on the aircraft catches the wire, bringing the aircraft very quickly to a halt. If the pilot misses the hook, he still has enough forward speed left to take off and try again. He will steer onto the angled flight deck, which is used only for taking off, and avoid the catch net on the main flight deck.

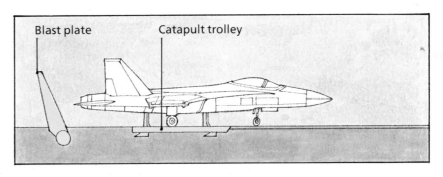

Blast plate   Catapult trolley

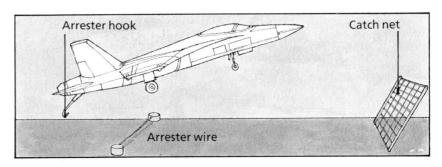

Arrester hook   Catch net

Arrester wire

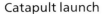

Anti-aircraft Defense

Both land forces and ships at sea need to be able to defend themselves against air attack, especially as friendly aircraft will never be able to stop every enemy aircraft and missile from getting through. Airfields, too, must be defended. Anti-aircraft weapons are either guns or missiles and can vary in size from a soldier's rifle to large missiles capable of engaging strategic bombers flying at high altitude.

Ship-borne systems

Ships rely very much more on missile systems than on guns for anti-aircraft defense because aircraft tend to make their attacks at a distance from the ship. As on land, the systems can either be point defense weapons, protecting the ship only or area weapons, protecting the whole task force.

Even more crucial at sea is the ability a point defense system to hit a missile coming toward it. The British Sea Wolf is very good for this because it was designed originally to hit a naval 4.5in shell in flight. It is radar-guided, but uses a television tracker to deal with very low level missiles like Exocet. Area defense systems have much longer ranges; typical of these is the US General Dynamics Standard missile system, which can engage targets up to 45km (28 miles) away. The emphasis at the longer range is to engage the aircraft, while point defense systems concentrate

more on the anti-missile role. Should an aircraft decide to make an attack at close range, then rapid-firing guns can be brought into play. Passive defense measures such as chaff dispensers, which can be launched by helicopters with the help of ship-borne radar, will also decoy the missile target.

Land-based systems

Frontline troops can use their personal weapons to engage enemy aircraft, while many of their armored vehicles have machine guns fitted specifically for air defense. They can also use a wide range of hand-held surface-to-air missile systems, like the Soviet SAM-7, American Stinger and British Blowpipe missiles. These have a horizontal range of 3000-5000m (9300-16,400ft) and a vertical range of up to 2000m (6560ft) and are also fitted with IFF devices. However, both these missiles and small arms rely for their effectiveness on the quick reaction of the operator, who will seldom have the time to spot a low-flying jet traveling at high speed before it has passed overhead and gone out of sight. Against slow-flying helicopters, of course, they will have more chance.

To engage low level jet fighters successfully, radar is needed; there are a number of mobile gun systems available mounted on tracked vehicles, which incorporate their own radar systems. The

Ship-borne defense systems in action :
1 Exocet sea-skimming anti-ship missile
2 Sea Dart, lightweight anti-aircraft and anti-missile surface-to-surface defense

3 Chaff dispensing decoy missile
4 Sea King helicopter with Airborne Early Warning system

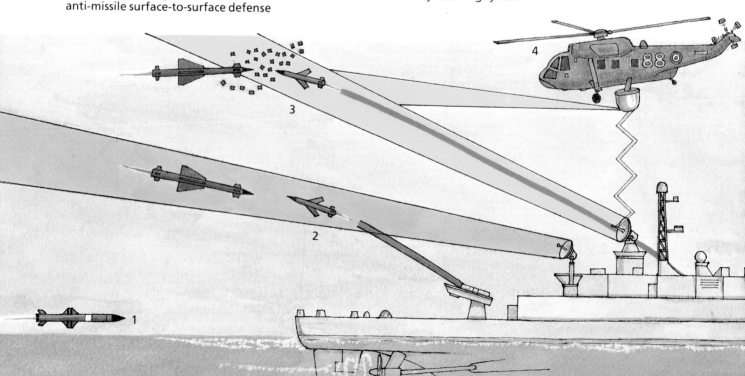

well proven Soviet ZSU 23-4 is a good example. It has four 23mm cannon in a large turret mounted on a PT-76 amphibious light tank chassis. The guns have a rate of fire of 4000 rounds per minute and can engage aircraft 3000m (9800ft) away. Once the radar has spotted an aircraft it automatically locks the guns onto it and keeps them on the target. This type of weapon is found in the front line of the battle.

Avoiding mistakes

To engage aircraft at higher altitudes, above 5000m (16,400ft), air defense systems consist almost entirely of missiles. These are often integrated with both Airborne Early Warning aircraft and ground radars. The most modern type is the US Patriot, which can shoot down both aircraft and missiles 45km (28 miles) away.

Air defense on land is divided between point and area defense weapons. The former means guarding a particular point like a vital bridge or headquarters, while the latter means protecting friendly troops in a particular area. Strict rules of engagement have to be laid down, especially if IFF devices are not working, to minimize the chances of shooting down friendly aircraft. Pilots are always nervous about flying over even friendly troops who can be understandably "trigger happy." Because of the grave threat from air defenses, it becomes understandable why many air-to-surface missiles home in on radar emissions. If the radars are knocked out, the air defense system becomes powerless.

U.S. Stinger shoulder-launched anti-aircraft missile

5 Attacking aircraft
6 Radome
7 General Dynamics Standard
   anti-missile missiles

The Future?

Like everything else, aviation technology does not stand still, and scientists and designers are forever looking for new methods of making the aircraft and its weapons even more effective. There are three particular areas which are being actively explored at present, and which are likely to bring concrete results before the end of the century.

Agile combat aircraft

Much effort is being made to design a new breed of fighter for the 1990s. Many countries agree that it should be a fighter first and a ground attack aircraft second. Above all it should be highly maneuverable, or agile, and a number of ideas are being developed to make it so. In order to reduce drag, the concept is being considered of mounting variable geometry tailplanes forward of the wings. These are called canards. In addition to altering the sweep of the wings, it is now possible to alter their cross-section shape or "camber," which again reduces drag and increases lift in certain conditions. By the same token, the engine air intakes can be made adjustable to ensure that the maximum amount of air is drawn in at a certain speed. Twin-tail fin rudders are already used on some aircraft, notably the US F-14 Tomcat and F-18 Hornet, as a means of improving stability. New materials for building the aircraft, such as carbon fibers, will make it lighter.

The pilot will be able to turn more tightly at higher speeds without feeling the physical effects. Many of the control surfaces will be able to adjust automatically. The new fighter will be faster and more agile, as well as smaller.

Stealth

The main aim of the US Stealth technology program is to produce an aircraft which offers the smallest possible chance of radar detection. This can be done by subtly modifying the aircraft's shape, by making the aircraft's skin of materials which reduce radar reflections and especially by the use of ever more sophisticated electronic systems to blind enemy radar. Engines too can be adapted to give off little or no infrared radiation to attract heat-seeking missiles. The US Air Force, in particular, are hard at work in this field and are planning to introduce a stealth bomber, which may well look like a flying wing with a delta shape.

Unmanned aerial platforms

Some commanders wish to make the RPV a weapons platform in itself, capable of dispensing precision guided sub-munitions. It is highly unlikely, however, that the human pilot will be wholly replaced by a computer. The latter may be able to think more quickly and store more information, but it lacks the flexibility and sheer inspiration of the human brain, which is often so important in war.

RPVs

Remote Patrol Vehicles, or drones, come in many shapes and sizes. Their primary use is for surveillance.

ML Aviation "Sprite" RPV

Israeli Aircraft Industries "Scout" RPV

Combat Aircraft
History and Development

The History of Combat Aircraft

Aircraft first entered the theater of war over the battlefields of northern France in 1914. Their primary role was in reconnaissance, but air crews soon armed themselves with rifles, pistols and grenades, and before long, machine guns. The Fokker Monoplane was the first to have a front mounted machine gun which fired between the blades of its spinning propeller. When it entered service in 1915 it swept the skies of Allied aircraft. The First World War also saw the beginning of another role for aircraft in combat – that of the strategic bomber. Germany made the first raids on London in 1917, and the British and French quickly retaliated.

The inter-war years

During the 1920s, aircraft were developed to fly even higher and faster. The potential of the strategic bomber to terrorize civilian populations led many military thinkers to believe that air forces would dominate any future confrontation.

In the 1930s, Germany, under Hitler, began a massive re-armament program. The German High Command had evolved a new strategy of warfare, the *Blitzkrieg*, or "lightening war." This envisaged a combined high speed attack by ground and air forces, striking deep into enemy territory and paralyzing his lines of supply and communication. Key to this role was the Ju87 Stuka dive-bomber.

The Second World War

Blitzkrieg tactics enabled Germany to take Poland, Denmark, Norway, the Low Countries and France in the early months of the war, and it now turned its attention on Britain. In August 1940 the battle for air supremacy over the Channel began. Spitfires and Hurricanes of the British Fighter Command inflicted crippling losses on the German Heinkel and Dornier bombers, and on the Me 109s and 110s that escorted them. By mid-September Germany had had enough, and it concentrated its attention to night attacks on British cities.

As the war progressed, so did the pace of technological advance. Radar, developed in strictest secrecy by the British in 1938, was mounted on the Mosquito nightfighter, to intercept German bombing raids. Long-range heavy payload bombers such as the B17 and Lancaster continued to inflict damage on German cities. In 1944 the first jets, the Gloster Meteor and the Me 262 went into service, and the Americans introduced the P-51 Mustang long-range fighter, probably the most successful propeller-driven fighter of the war.

In the Pacific, it was a war of aircraft carriers. The Japanese attack on Pearl Harbor, itself one of the most devastating examples of the effectiveness of air strike capability, had missed America's carriers which were at sea when the attack came.

The end of the war

Air power played a major role in the Allied invasion of France in 1944, and the bombing campaign against Germany lasted right up until the last days of the war in Europe. A few months later, across the other side of the world, the world saw the arrival of a new and even more terrifying face of war when American B-29s dropped atomic bombs on the Japanese cities of Hiroshima and Nagasaki.

The age of electronics

In post-war years there have been conflicts in Korea, Vietnam and the Middle East in which new aviation technologies could be tested. Electronics, in the form of radars and other detection systems, and in computer systems in the aircraft itself, have played an increasingly important part in shaping the modern combat aircraft.

The two most recent developments increase the flexibility of the combat aircraft in battle: swing-wings enable high performance in a variety of roles, and V/STOL jets such as the Harrier can operate without the need for a conventional airfield. The short history that follows highlights some of the most important aircraft in aviation history.

BE2 *(1913, Great Britain)*
In the years leading up to the outbreak of World War I in 1914 all the major nations formed military air wings. The aircraft used were designed solely for reconnaissance and typical of these was the British BE2, which was designed at the Royal Aircraft Factory. It had a crew of two – pilot and observer – and had a single water-cooled, gasoline-driven engine. It had a top speed of 110km/h (68mph), a height ceiling of 3000m (9800ft) and could stay airborne for some three hours. On September 22, 1914 it took part in the first bombing raid of the war, when four aircraft of No. 3 Squadron Royal Naval Air Service set out to attack the Zeppelin airship sheds at Dusseldorf and Cologne. Although by mid-1915 it had become easy prey for faster and better armed German fighters, it stayed in service as a reconnaissance plane until well into 1917.

Morane-Saulnier L *(1914, France)*
Most World War I combat aircraft were biplanes, but one or two early models were single wing, or monoplanes, as they were called. Examples of these are the German Taube and French Morane-Saulnier. Nicknamed the Parasol by the British, because of the way it was rigged, it had a top speed of just over 110km/h (68mph) and could operate up to a height of 4300m (14,100ft). It had some success as a fighter in early 1915, when the French air ace Roland Garros arranged for deflector plates to be fitted on his propeller to enable him to fire a forward machine gun through it, or otherwise the propeller would have been shattered. The first air Victoria Cross was also won on this aircraft when Sub. Lt. Warneford destroyed a Zeppelin on June 7, 1915 by dropping bombs on it. Like the BE2, the Morane Parasol was soon overtaken by faster fighter types.

Vickers FB5 Gunbus
(1915, Great Britain)
The British solution to the forward-firing machine gun problem was

BE2

initially to mount the engine at the rear and place the observer in front of the pilot so that he could have an uninterrupted forward field of fire. This design was called a "pusher" as opposed to a "tractor" which had the engine mounted at the front of the fuselage. The Gunbus design had originally been drawn up in 1912 in response to an Admiralty requirement for an aircraft mounting a machine gun, but not until the late summer of 1915 did it see combat in France. Although its top speed was 110km/h (68mph) only and it was limited to operating below 3000m (9800ft), it shot down several German aircraft in the latter part of 1915.

Fokker E *(1915, Germany)*
This was another monoplane, but it swung the air war over the Western Front in favor of the Germans. Designed by the young Dutchman Anthony Fokker, it owed its success to having a speed in excess of 120km/h (75mph) and a new solution to the forward-firing machine gun. When Roland Garros was shot down in April 1915, the Germans noted his deflector plates, and Fokker's design team evolved what was called an interrupter gear. This synchronized the propeller with the machine gun so that the bullets passed through it without hitting the blades. From mid-1915 it began to build up a large score of French and British victims. In

all, although only some 300 were built, they accounted for more than 1000 Allied aircraft in what was dubbed the "Fokker Scourge." Fokker continued to produce excellent fighter aircraft during the war and these, along with the Pfalz and Albatross and other types, enabled the German Air Force to fight fiercely right up to the end of the war. The other very famous Fokker design was the Triplane flown by Baron Von Richthofen, the Red Baron.

SPAD *(1916, France)*
Designed and built by the French firm of Societé Anonyme Pour l'Aviation et ses Dérivés, after whose initials the aircraft was named, the Spad was one of the most successful fighters of World War I. The Spad VII began its operational career in Autumn 1916 and did much to restore French fortunes in the air war. It was a single-seater, armed with two forward-firing machine guns and had a top speed of 190km/h (118mph) and a service ceiling of 5500m (18,000ft). Such was its popularity that almost every Allied air force was equipped with it, and it won particular renown with the crack French squadron *Les Cicognes* (The Storks). Later in the war it was superseded by the more powerful Spad XIII, with a top speed of 200km/h (124mph), and this became the mainstay of the American aviation arm in France in 1918.

SPAD

Bristol Fighter

Sopwith Triplane
(1916, Great Britain)

By mid-1916 it was becoming clear to designers that a successful fighter required not just speed and height, speed and maneuverability. Then, it climb in order to get above enemy aircraft, thereby giving the best chance of shooting them down. The British firm of Sopwith believed that this could be done by building an aircraft with three wings, thereby giving additional lift. When it arrived on the Western Front in early 1917, its rate of climb of 400m (1300ft) per minute far exceeded that of any other service aircraft of the time, so much so that many German fighter firms quickly began to bring out triplanes as well, although only the Fokker Dr.1 was widely used. The Sopwith itself was not produced in large quantities, being quickly replaced by the Sopwith Camel biplane, which was as successful as the Spad and extremely popular among Allied pilots.

Bristol Fighter *(1916, Great Britain)*

Another solution to the "Fokker Scourge" was this two-seater fighter affectionately called the Brisfit. It had the advantage of being more heavily armed than single-seater types, with the observer covering the rear with one or two 0.303 Lewis guns and the pilot having a fixed forward-firing Vickers as well as a flexible Lewis mounted on the top wing. It arrived on the Western Front at the beginning of April 1917, a month when the Germans gained temporary air superiority over the Royal Flying Corps, who nicknamed this time "Bloody April." The Brisfit also suffered until pilots began to appreciate its speed and maneuverability. Then, it quickly established a high reputation, and the Germans produced similar two-seaters in the Hannover and Halberstadt. It was a brave single-seater pilot who would take on a two-seater fighter on his own. The Brisfit continued in RAF service throughout the 1920s, especially in the Middle East.

Gotha G.IV *(1917, Germany)*

Although the Germans had been intermittently attacking England with Zeppelins since 1915, a new development in air warfare took place in the early summer of 1917 when aircraft began bombing raids on the south of England, culminating in attacks on London itself. This produced some panic among the civilian population, and was to lead to retaliatory raids against Germany by the British and French, and the beginning of the belief that bombers could win wars almost on their own by attacking civilian morale. This first strategic bomber, the Gotha G.IV, was the latest in a series which had made its first flight in January 1915. It was powered by two 260hp engines, which drove it at a maximum speed of just under 160km/h (99mph), and it could carry 500kg (1100lbs) of bombs over a range of 850km (528 miles).

Sopwith Triplane

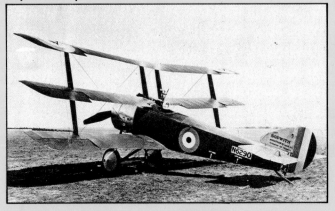

Gotha G.IV

Sopwith Camel (1917, Britain)

With the distinction of destroying more enemy aircraft than any other type in World War I, the Camel was perhaps the most famous fighter of that war. A natural development of the Sopwith Pup and Triplane, it reached the Front in July 1917 and remained in operational service for the rest of the war. It was on this aircraft and its sister, the SE5, that most British and Commonwealth aces won their spurs. Although many pilots favored the latter type because she was easier to fly, she was not as nimble as the Camel, whose rotary engine enabled her to make a very swift right turn, which German pilots learned to their cost in dogfights. Nevertheless, in inexperienced hands, she could spin very easily and many lives were lost in her because of this. She was very versatile, performing very effectively in the ground attack role ("trench strafing") and as a naval fighter, taking off from early aircraft carriers.

Sopwith Camel

Vickers Vimy (1918, Britain)

In retaliation for the Gotha raids on London, the British began to design heavy bombers with the object of attacking Berlin. The firms of Handley-Page and Vickers both produced types which came into service just before the end of the war, but too late for attacks on Berlin to be mounted. The Vickers Vimy had a crew of three and the final version had two 460hp engines. It could fly at just over 160km/h (99mph) and carry 2200kg (4850lbs) of bombs 1600km (995 miles). In June 1919 Alcock and Brown became the first to fly an aircraft across the Atlantic non-stop, taking sixteen hours to do it in their Vickers Vimy. She also took Ross and Keith Smith in November of that year on the first flight from England to Australia which, with stops for refueling, took 133 hours. These flights marked the beginning of the era of pioneering long distance flights which dominated the Twenties and early Thirties and rapidly increased the speed of world communications.

Vickers Virginia (1924, Britain)

A successor to the Vimy, the Virginia was the Royal Air Force's main heavy bomber for most of the period between the two world wars. Although she had a performance little better than that of the Vimy, she was an improvement in other ways. Apart from the open cockpit, the positions of the other crew members were enclosed in the fuselage. Later versions also had a metal structure, as opposed to wood, and an autopilot. The Virginia and the later Vickers Wellesley, which was a monoplane, helped maintain the RAF's belief in the long-range bomber as a decisive weapon of war. The RAF put this to the test in World War Two, in bombers like the Lancaster and Halifax.

Curtiss Hawk (1924, USA)

Originally designed by the US firm of Curtiss as a single-seater fighter, the Hawk had a number of revolutionary features. A new design of water-cooled engine gave it a new shape of streamlined nose and a speed of well over 300km/h (186mph). The Goshawk of 1932 was a direct derivative of the Hawk, and was designed as a dive bomber, the first ever, and had metal wings and retractable landing wheels. It was this aircraft which inspired the Germans to produce the JU 87 Stuka (see p. 38). Another generation of Hawks – Mohawk, Tomahawk and Kittihawk among them – saw much service as fighters and fighter bombers during World War Two.

Vickers Vimy

Fiat CR.32 (1933, Italy)

The Italian Fiat Company had been producing fighters since the early 1920s, and the CR.32 was to form the mainstay of the Italian Air Force of the late Thirties. Although a biplane, its all metal construction and streamlined fuselage gave it a speed of over 360km/h (224mph) and a service ceiling of almost 10,000m (32,800ft). Like many fighters of the time it owed much in design to the annual Schneider Trophy speed competitions. A number fought on the Nationalist side in the Spanish Civil War.

Heinkel He51 (1934, Germany)

The Germans had been restricted by the Peace Treaty of 1919 from building military aircraft, but did begin to develop a new breed during the Twenties under the guise of civil aviation. By the time Hitler came to power in 1933, the He51 was ready for unveiling. Like the Fiat CR.32 it was a biplane with open cockpit, but lacked its speed, maximum 300km/h (186mph), and service ceiling, 8000m (24,600ft). Nevertheless, it was useful enough for its day, and was the first fighter ordered for the Luftwaffe. It saw service during the Spanish Civil War.

Polikarpov I-16 (1934, Russia)

Russia had a thriving aircraft industry by 1914, but the Revolution of three years later, and the Civil War which followed, halted its activities for a time. Then, under Stalin it quickly began to gather momentum again, and the I-16 was one of the results of this. Its stubby "homemade" appearance belied its performance, as CR.32 and He51 pilots discovered to their cost during the Spanish Civil War. With a top speed of some 400km/h (250mph) and a rate of climb of almost 1000m (3280ft) per minute, this single-seat monoplane, some models with an enclosed cockpit, was a remarkably robust little fighter. Although outdated by 1941, the Russians continued to use it in large numbers until 1943, to hold off the German onslaught. During this period of the air war, quantity was more important than quality.

Junkers Ju 52 (1934, Germany)

This began life as the main civilian airliner of Lufthansa, the national German airline, but, as with many other types developed by Germany during the late Twenties and early Thirties, it had always been intended for military purposes. Originally it was planned as both a bomber and transport, and equipped the first Luftwaffe bombing squadron, but better bombers like the Ju 88 and He 111 (see below) soon replaced it. As a transport, it became very much a "maid of all work" and served on every front on which the Germans fought. It could carry some 600kg (1320lbs) over 1200km (745 miles), and was very sturdy and reliable. In all, almost 5000 were built, and some remained in service with the Spanish Air Force until as late as 1975.

Heinkel He111 (1936, Germany)

One of Hitler's major mistakes of World War Two was to build medium as opposed to heavy bombers. He did this in the belief that fast, lighter bombers could evade fighters and also because he envisaged war only with his immediate neighbors. The results were the He111, Ju 88 and Do 17. They were all two-engined aircraft, and the He111 especially, when it first made its appearance, was impressive with its top speed of 400km/h (250mph), although with a full bomb load of 2000kg (4400lbs) this was reduced to just over 320km/h (200mph) and its range to 1150 km (715 miles). The Spanish Civil War seem to bear out the belief that it could evade fighters, but against the modern Hurricane and Spitfire during the Battle of Britain in 1940 it proved an easy victim. Efforts were made to increase its armor and defensive armament and the crew grew from four to six members. The result was that it merely became cumbersome.

Bristol Blenheim (1936, Britain)

The British, too, were attracted to the idea of the faster, lighter bomber in the mid-1930s. It was also generally held that there was no effective means of preventing enemy bombers from attacking Britain, at least not until radar, which could give early warning of their approach, was developed in the latter half of the decade. The only answer seemed to be to match the Germans in quantities of aircraft in order to deter them, and light/medium bombers could be built in greater numbers than heavier types. The three-seat Blenheim, although it could carry only 500kg (1100lbs) of bombs, was faster with a much greater range than the He111, and many countries bought them. Yet, when war came it proved just as vulnerable to fighters as the He111 and, as a day bomber, was subsequently replaced by better US types like the Boston and Mitchell. Many were converted to night-fighters and had some success in this role until replaced by the Mosquito.

Heinkel He111

Junkers Ju 87 Stuka

(1937, Germany)

One of the key elements of the German Blitzkrieg attacks of 1939-42 was the use of the Stuka dive bomber. With the scream of its specially fitted siren as it dived to the attack, it caused terror among many ground troops. The Germans originally obtained the dive bomber idea from the US Curtiss Goshawk (p. 36) and, equipped with machine guns and one 500kg (1100lb) and four 50kg (110lb) bombs slung beneath its fuselage and wings, it was a formidable ground attack weapon. It could dive at as much as 10° vertically but, because of the tendency of pilots to black out when pulling out of the dive, a form of autopilot had to be fitted. During the Battle of Britain it was used as a conventional bomber but its relatively slow horizontal speed was no match for the Hurricanes and Spitfires of British Fighter Command. Mounting two 37mm cannon, it did go on to become a highly successful "tank buster" on the Eastern Front.

Messerschmidt Me 109

(1937, Germany)

During the late Thirties all the major aircraft-producing countries finally gave up the biplane fighter in favor of the monoplane. Thus the German Air Force replaced its He 51s with what was to become one of the most famous fighters of all time, the Me 109. When it first entered service it was, with a top speed of just under 450km/h (280mph), the fastest fighter in the world and this, and its three forward firing machine guns, made it a force to be reckoned with. During the early years of the war only the Spitfire could match it, and an intense rivalry built up between the two, with each going through several modifications. By 1945, the Me 109K could reach speeds of 700km/h (435mph), and although the later Focke-Wulf Fw 190 was faster and carried more punch, the Me 109 still flew on in large numbers.

Messerschmidt Me 109

Supermarine Spitfire *(1938, Britain)*

Certainly the most famous British combat aircraft of all time, the Spitfire was the RAF's answer to the Me 109. Designed by Mitchell, a dying man, it was Britain's first all-metal stressed-skin fighter and arrived just in time to join its slightly older sister, the Hawker Hurricane, in defending the country against the threatened German invasion of 1940. With radar and the skill and bravery of the pilots, they denied Hitler air supremacy. The Spitfire appeared in several different versions.

Short S.25 Sunderland

(1938, Britain)

Flying boats, which could take off and land on water, had been developed prior to World War One and saw much service with naval forces during that war. Between the wars they became the main means of opening up trans-ocean air routes, with designers concentrating on increasing range and endurance. The Sunderland was one of the most famous. Powered by four engines, it had a slow maximum speed of some 340km/h (210mph) but a range of almost 4830km (3000 miles).

Supermarine Spitfire

Vickers-Armstrong Wellington
(1938, Britain)
This was undoubtedly the best of the two-engine bombers with which the RAF went to war in 1939. Designed as a long-range bomber, it was of an unusual geodetic construction, whereby the metal framework gave the appearance of basketwork. This concept had been used by the famous designer Barnes Wallis in airship construction, and made the Wellington a remarkably robust and tough aircraft which could take much punishment, but still keep flying. Initially, the RAF concentrated on bombing by day, but none of its aircraft had sufficient armament to keep the German fighters at bay and it was forced to operate by night. The Wellington had a crew of six and a range of over 3000km (1864 miles) with a 700kg (1540lb) bomb load, flying at speeds up to 450km/h (280mph). Although it was no longer used as a bomber by the end of 1943, being replaced by heavier types, it continued to serve as an anti-submarine aircraft and trainer, and remained in the latter role until 1953.

Boeing B-17 Flying Fortress
(1939, USA)
The most notable US bomber of World War Two, the B-17 was originally designed to protect the USA against enemy fleets, but its worth as a long-range bomber was soon realized. Its first combat experience was, however, with the RAF before the USA entered the war. The Americans believed that using it with the Norden bombsight, they could bomb accurately, something the RAF found difficult to do. The RAF tried to use it in 1941, but found that it did not have sufficient armament. The Americans increased this, and the result was the B-17E which bore the bulk of their bombing effort against Germany. Its four engines drove it at speeds of almost 450km/h (280mph) and it could fly 1700km (1056 miles) with a maximum bomb load of 6 tonnes (5.9 tons). It was armed with no less

Vickers-Armstrong Wellington

than thirteen machine guns, and had a crew of up to ten. Although its armament was impressive it still suffered in daylight raids against Germany, and only the introduction of the P-51 long-range escort fighter would reduce its losses.

Handley Page Halifax
(1940, Britain)
Although during the Thirties the RAF had tried to match the Germans in numbers rather than quality of bombers, specifications were drawn up in 1936 for a new breed of heavy bombers in the belief that the

bombing of Germany might well prove decisive if and when war came. These became the Short Stirling, Avro Manchester and Halifax, and it was the last named which proved the most successful. It had a crew of seven and could carry 6 tonnes (5.9 tons) of bombs 1500km (932 miles) and was capable of speeds up to 400km/h (248.5mph). It underwent a number of modifications during the war and although used as a bomber throughout, also found employment as a glider tug, transport, paratroop-carrier and electronics counter-measures platform.

Boeing B-17 Flying Fortress

Mitsubishi A6M Zero-Sen

Consolidated Vultee Liberator

Mitsubishi A6M Zero-Sen
(1940, Japan)
Before Japan entered the war at the end of 1941, there was a general belief in Western eyes that she was incapable of producing modern combat aircraft, yet alone flying them effectively. It therefore came as a shock to the Americans and British in the Pacific when they came up against the carrier-based Zero fighter. With a speed well in excess of 450km/h (280mph), and a rate of climb of 1500m (4920ft) per minute, as well as being highly maneuverable, it outclassed existing Allied fighters. Using drop tanks, it also had an unbelievable range of 3000km (1864 miles).

De Havilland Mosquito
(1941, Britain)
This aircraft was the result of a private venture to design a high-speed, unarmed day bomber made of wood in order to ease the strain on Britain's aircraft metal suppliers. Considering wooden aircraft now out of date, the Air Ministry initially showed little enthusiasm. Not until a prototype flew at the end of 1940 did they change their minds, and one of the most versatile aircraft of the war entered service. It could operate at heights well above 10,000m (32,800ft), at speeds of up to 650km/h (405mph) and to a range, in its reconnaissance version, of 4700km (2930 miles). Crewed by a pilot and navigator, it was also highly maneuverable. Besides long-range reconnaissance, it acted as a light bomber, fighterbomber, night fighter and carrierborne aircraft, and was especially effective against pinpoint targets. It was also used to attack enemy shipping, and to mark targets for heavy bombers.

Consolidated Vultee Liberator
(1941, USA)
Another significant US aircraft of World War Two, the Liberator saw service in many theaters of war. Originally conceived as a heavy bomber, it was developed somewhat later than its rival, the B-17, and was much more sophisticated, although more difficult to fly. Like the latter, it was heavily-armed and had a crew of ten in the bomber role, and could carry 2.5 tonnes (2.4 tons) of bombs some 3500km (2200 miles). Used by the RAF as well as the Americans, it also operated as a transport. It was, however, as an anti-submarine aircraft that it made its greatest impact, and it made a significant contribution to the final winning of the battle of the Atlantic in Spring 1943. Indicative of how popular an aircraft it was during the war, is that 19,200 aircraft were built.

North American P-51 Mustang
(1941, USA)
The initiative for the introduction of this, one of the most successful US fighters, actually came from the RAF, who commissioned North American Aviation in April 1940 to produce a new fighter for them. They received some 800 Mustangs, and the US Army Air Force, seeing what a good aircraft it was, also placed orders. The version which really made its mark was the P-51D, which had an operational range (which meant that it could fight en route), of 2090km (1300 miles). It could thus give the US bombers protection for their daylight raids deep into Germany. Its top speed of 695km/h (430mph) and maneuverability also enabled it to cope with the German fighters.

De Havilland Mosquito

North American P-51 Mustang

Avro Lancaster

Ilyushin IL-2 Stormovik
(1942, Russia)

When the Germans invaded the Soviet Union in June 1941, the Soviet Air Force found itself burdened with obsolete types which were no match for the Luftwaffe. The Russians quickly learned their lesson and one of the first new models to appear was the IL-2 Stormovik. Essentially a ground attack aircraft, it was also capable of shooting down German fighters. Equipped with cannon, rockets and bombs, it came in single and two-seat versions. In the latter case an air gunner sitting behind the pilot covered the rear. It normally operated at heights of 300m (980ft) and below and proved to be a valuable weapon in the land battle.

Republic P-47 Thunderbolt
(1942, USA)

This US fighter was designed very much after digesting the lessons of the early part of World War Two. Its big and powerful 2,800hp engine made it large for a fighter, and the shape of the engine cowling made it difficult for the pilot to see forward. When taxiing he normally had to have someone sitting on the wing to guide him. Once in the air, however, with its top speed of well over 600km/h (373mph) and its high operating ceiling of above 13,000m (42,650ft), as well as its eight wing-mounted machine guns, it was a formidable fighter. Carrying drop tanks it could, like the P-51, be used as a bomber escort, and the P-47D bomber version proved very successful both in Europe and the Pacific campaign.

Avro Lancaster *(1942, Britain)*

What the Spitfire was to RAF Fighter Command, the Lancaster was to RAF Bomber Command. It was a direct development from the Manchester, whose two engines were found to be unreliable. The addition of an extra two transformed the aircraft, and it was to become the backbone of the RAF's offensive against Germany. It had a crew of seven – pilot, engineer, navigator, wireless operator, bomb aimer, two gunners – and carried a normal bomb load of 7 tonnes (6.9 tons) 3100km (1660 miles). Lancasters were, however, modified toward the end of the war to carry a heavier loads. Indeed, no other World War Two bomber could carry such a load so far, and their loss rate was very much lower than the Halifax or Stirling. Lancasters took part in every major RAF bombing raid from 1942 onward, including the famous Dams Raid of May 1943 and the sinking of the *Tirpitz* in November 1944. Post-war developments of the Lancaster were the Lincoln bomber and the Shackleton maritime patrol and airborne early warning aircraft, which was still in front-line RAF service in the 1980s.

Boeing B-29 Superfortress
(1943, USA)

The largest bomber of World War Two, the B-29 was able to deliver 5 tonnes (4.9 tons) of bombs to a distance of no less than 4500km (2800 miles). It spearheaded the American bombing offensive against mainland Japan from 1944 onward, operating from bases in the Marianas. Its greatest claim to fame was that it was used to drop the atom bomb on Hiroshima and Nagasaki in August 1945. For a moment it looked as though the pre-war air theorists' belief that the bomber could win wars on its own might after all have been proved. The advent of the nuclear missile quickly dispelled this.

Boeing B-29 Superfortress

Gloster (later Hawker Siddeley) Meteor *(1944, Britain)*

The Meteor has already been mentioned earlier in this book as the first jet aircraft to see action, when it first appeared in the skies over England in July 1944. Its first task was not, however, as a fighter but as a means of countering the German flying bombs, either by shooting them down or by putting them off course by tipping them over by their wing tips. It soon developed a top speed of 900km/h (560mph), far in excess of any piston aircraft, and could operate at heights of up to 15,000m (49,200ft). Its rate of climb was also quickly improved from a mere 700m (2300ft) to 2000m (6560ft) per minute. Night-fighter and reconnaissance versions were also developed, and it remained in service, especially as a trainer, until the 1960s. It also sold widely abroad.

Messerschmidt Me 262
(1944, Germany)

Although the Me 262 made its first flight in April 1941, it was to be over three years before it first appeared in combat because of lack of official interest and Hitler's belief that it should be developed as a bomber rather than fighter. When it did finally arrive to defend German skies against the Allied onslaught in late summer 1944, it gave the British and Americans much cause for concern. Its top speed of 800km/h (497mph) exceeded that of the early Meteor, and its rate of climb of almost 1300m (4265ft) per minute made it ideal as an air defense fighter. Although a beautiful aircraft to fly, its engines were very unreliable and its short endurance time also acted against it. Nevertheless, by the end of the war it had claimed many successes and well over 1400 had been built.

North American F-86 Sabre
(1947, USA)

The Americans were somewhat later entering the jet aircraft era than the British and Germans, but when they did, they produced an aircraft which

Messerschmidt Me 262

quickly gained a very high world-wide reputation. It could fly at 1100km/h (684mph) and won its spurs in Korea, where it proved itself to be superior to all other fighters except the MiG-15 (see below). Such was its success, that it became the standard fighter of many air forces in the 1950s.

Mikoyan MiG-15 *(1948, Russia)*

Just as the Zero had caused such a sensation among Allied pilots in the Pacific, so did the MiG-15 when United Nations pilots came up against it in Korea. Its swept wings and engine copied from the Rolls-Royce Nene turbojet engine gave it a speed of almost 1100km/h (684mph) and a very high rate of climb of over 3000m (9840ft) per minute, much in excess of the early Sabres. It outflew the majority of UN aircraft and its maneuverability was also better than that of the Sabre. Only the inexperience of its hastily trained Chinese and North Korean pilots counted against it, but this was enough to give the UN forces overall air superiority. It marked the first in a series of MiG fighters which would prove ever more sophisticated and effective.

Boeing B-52 Stratofortress
(1955, USA)

The largest bomber ever built, the B-52 has been one of the major nuclear and conventional weapons systems in the US armory for over

25 years. Originally designed with a straight wing and turboprop engine in 1946, the development of a suitable turbojet by Pratt & Witney enabled a swept wing shape to be adopted. Powered by eight of these engines, the B-52 is able to operate at heights of 18,000m (59,000ft) flying at 900km/h (560mph). It can carry no less than 30 tonnes (29.5 tons) of bombs stowed internally and externally, and with this load fly over 8500km (5282 miles). It can also carry a variety of missiles. It was widely used in Vietnam and its ability to saturate a small area with bombs literally changed the shape of the map in parts of that country. It will gradually be replaced by the Rockwell B-1B.

Tupolev Tu-20 (NATO Codename "Bear") *(1956, Russia)*

The Russians, too, were quick to develop strategic bombers with a nuclear capability in the years after 1945. Among these were the Tu-16 Badger, a turbojet, and the Bear, a turboprop. The Bear is unable to carry the load of the B-52 and has a lower top speed. Nevertheless, this is balanced by its superior range of 12,000km (7460 miles). The Bear B carries the AS-3 Kangaroo stand-off missile system, with a 600km (372 miles) range, and other versions have been designed for maritime patrol work. The latest variant is the Moss, an Airborne Warning and Control System aircraft like the E-3A.

Hawker Siddeley Vulcan

Lockheed C-130 Hercules
(1956, USA)
This is one of the most successful military aircraft ever built. It was designed as a result of the US experience during the Berlin Airlift of winter 1948-9 – when the Russians sealed off West Berlin and the civil population was entirely reliant on aircraft for supply of living essentials – and in Korea. A requirement was produced for an aircraft which could operate on rough strips and transport 10 tonnes (9.8 tons) of stores or 92 infantrymen/64 paratroopers over 3000km (1860 miles). The C-130 was the result, and very quickly impressed USAF pilots by its superb handling characteristics, which many likened to those of a fighter. Affectionately called the "Herky Bird" by the Americans, the C-130 is now in service with over fifty nations, with a number of variants including air tankers, gunships and spacecraft tracking and retrieval. It has a normal crew of four, and although its four turboprop engines are very noisy for passengers, this is more than made up for by its reliability.

Lockheed U-2 *(1956, USA)*
The U-2 Spyplane has already been mentioned in the Intelligence section of the book. Although it has been partially replaced in service by the Lockheed SR-71 Blackbird, it still remains in service, nearly thirty years after it flew its first missions.

It has a comparatively low top speed of just over 750km/h (466mph), but the key to its success is its ability to operate at heights of well over 27,000m (85,580ft) and to remain airborne for some eight hours.

Hawker Siddeley Vulcan
(1958, Britain)
This was the last of the so-called V-bombers to enter RAF service after the Valiant and Victor. These provided the means of delivering Britain's strategic nuclear weapon until this role was taken over by the Polaris submarine. The Vulcan was the best of the three, with its delta wing shape giving it remarkable maneuverability for its large size. It was powered by four turbojets, and had a crew of five. Its maximum speed was just under 800km/h (497mph) with an initial 4500km (2800 mile) range, later increased to 7500km (4660 miles). It served in the RAF until 1983 and will be remembered for its attacks on Port Stanley airfield during the 1982 Falklands campaign.

General Dynamics F-111
(1967, USA)
The original intention behind this aircraft was to produce a fighter which would suit both USAF and US Navy needs, but technical problems during development resulted in the cancellation of the carrier version. Its initial poor reputation was also not

helped by the quick loss of three out of the first six sent to Vietnam, all as a result of a faulty weld in the tailplane. Even so, as the first swing-wing or variable geometry aircraft to enter service, it did eventually turn out to be a first-class combat aircraft in both the fighter and bomber roles. Its top speed of Mach 2.5 at 13,000m (42,650ft) and ability to fly at 60m (197ft) at Mach 1.2, thanks to its advanced avionics, makes it a very versatile aircraft, and it is used both for tactical strike and as a strategic nuclear weapon delivery means, when its ability to fly beneath enemy radar cover is a particular advantage.

Hawker Siddeley Harrier
(1969, Britain)
In the 1950s designers began to realize that the thrust produced by the gas turbine engine made it possible to develop an aircraft capable of vertical takeoff and landing (VTOL). The VTOL prototype, the P.1127, was designed in the late Fifties and this gave way to the Kestrel from which the Harrier was evolved. Both land and carrier-borne versions exist, the former being used for close air support while the latter is multi-role. The US Marine Corps also uses it and calls it the AV-8A. One particular technique, "viffing" (vectoring in forward flight), which enables the Harrier to come to an immediate halt in midair, has made it very effective in dogfights, as shown in the Falklands campaign. An improved version, the AV-8B, is under joint development by the British and Americans.

Hawker Siddeley Nimrod
(1969, Britain)
The Nimrod is derived from the Comet airliner, the mainstay of British civil aviation in the 1950s. It was designed as a replacement to the Shackleton maritime patrol aircraft. To fly the aircraft there is a crew of three – two pilots and an air engineer – but up to nine additional crew members are carried in order to operate the surveillance and navigation equipment and to act as observers.

General Dynamics F-16 *(1978, USA)*

This originally started life as an investigation into the possibilities of producing a lightweight fighter without the expense of the F-15, which had been developed in a hurry to counter the Soviet MiG-25. By the early Seventies a number of European countries were beginning to look for replacements for their F-104 Starfighters and the F-16 seemed to fit the bill. Thus it was put into production and not only a large number of other countries bought it, but the USAF as well. Available as a one-seat air combat or two-seat interdiction aircraft, the F-16 has a reheat turbofan engine with a maximum speed of just over Mach 2. It is armed with a 20mm multi-barrel rotary cannon and can carry weapon loads up to a weight of 7 tonnes (6.9 tons).

Mikoyan MiG-25 (NATO Codename "Foxbat") *(1970, Russia)*

As with other Soviet aircraft, the MiG-25 caused a large stir in Western aviation circles when it was first seen. Indeed, the USA hurriedly designed the F-15 in order to counter it. It comes in two types, the Foxbat A, which is an interceptor, and the B and D reconnaissance versions. It is capable of speeds of almost Mach 3 at the higher altitudes and has an impressive rate of climb of over 13,000m (42,650ft) per minute. It is normally armed with four AA-6 Acrid air-to-air missiles. An advanced Foxbat is expected to enter service at any time, incorporating a radar system giving a look-down shoot-down capability, which will enable it to engage aircraft flying below it at low level.

Dassault-Breguet/Dornier Alpha Jet *(1978, France and Germany)*

This aircraft is a joint development by the French and Germans. Many advanced jet trainers are designed to have a secondary combat role, and may often be bought for the latter by poorer countries. The Alpha Jet is of interest in that the French wanted it

General Dynamics F-16

as a trainer while the Germans are using it as a light strike aircraft. This, however, has meant two different versions, a two-seater, to house pilot and instructor, for the French, and a German single-seater. Although its top speed is below Mach 1, it is highly maneuverable and very effective in both roles. It is armed with a 27mm or 30mm cannon and four fixed wing hardpoints for a variable external weapons load to a maximum weight of 2.5 tonnes (2.4 tons). It is gaining an excellent reputation among allies.

Panavia Tornado *(1981, Britain, Germany and Italy)*

Tornado has already been described in some detail earlier in the book. An important point which has not as yet been made, however, is that the high technology aircraft of today is very costly to develop and produce, and is getting beyond the pocket of all but the Superpowers. More and more, therefore, the smaller nations, especially European, are combining together in collaborative projects. This is often not as easy as it sounds, as each nation has slightly different requirements and differing replacement times for existing aircraft. Indicative of this is the production of the Tornado Air Defense Version for Britain only, in what is a tri-national project with the Germans and Italians. The latter use the Interdictor/Strike version of the Tornado, as do the RAF, of course.

Rockwell B-1B *(1986?, USA)*

The latest US strategic bomber emphasizes the continued US belief in what is called the "nuclear triad," the ability to launch strategic nuclear weapons from land, from under the sea, and from the air. Although smaller than the B-52, which it will eventually replace, the B-1B still looks large. Although prototypes have been flying since 1976, plans to build 240 to replace the B-52 were reversed in 1979. This was amended at the end of 1981 and 100 have been ordered, modified to take the Cruise nuclear missile in its air-launched configuration. The B-1B has a crew of four and can fly at over Mach 1.5 at 13,000m (42,650ft) and has a range of 8500km (5280 miles).

Combat Aircraft in Service Today

Country (and number of attack aircraft in service)	Strike/Attack, ground attack and Air Superiority aircraft	Strategic and Tactical Bombers	Reconnaissance and Airborne Early Warning Aircraft	Maritime patrol and Naval Strike aircraft	Transport aircraft
Algeria (210)	MiG-17; MiG-19; MiG-21; MiG-23; MiG-25; Su-7; Su-20; Magister	Il-28	MiG-25	F-27	An-12; C-130; Caravelle Il-18; Mystère-Falcom
Argentina (198)	A-4; Dagger; MS-760; Mirage III; Mirage 5; Pucara	Canberra		A-4; Super Etendard	Boeing 707; C-47; C-130; DHC-6; F-27; F-28; IA-50; Learjet 35-A; Merlin IV; Sabreliner; Turbo-Commander
Belgium (124)	F-16; F-104; Mirage 5		Mirage 5		Boeing 727; C-130; Falcon 20; HS-748; Merlin III
Brazil (54)	F-5; Mirage III		RC-95; T-26	P-95; S-2	AM-X; Boeing 737; C-47; C-130; DHC-5; EMB-110; EMB-120; EMB-810; HS-125
Canada	CF-116 (F-5); F-18; F-104			CP-121; CP-140	C-130; CC-109; CC-115 (DHC-5); CC-117; CC-137 (Boeing 707)
China (4,500)	A(Qiang)-5; F(Jian)-4; F-5; F-6; F-7; F-8; (MiG-23)	B-5 (Il-28); B-6 (Tu-16)	B-5; F-6		An-24; An-26; BAe Trident; Il-18; Li-2; Y-5 (An-2); Y-7; Y-8 (An-12)
Egypt (460)	Alphajet; F-4; Chinese F-6; F-16; MiG-17; MiG-21; Mirage 5; Mirage 2000; Su-7	Tu-16	MiG-21; Mirage 5; Su-7	Il-28	An-12; Boeing 707; Boeing 737; C-130; DHC-5; Falcon 20; Il-14
France (215)	Jaguar; Mirage III; Mirage F-1; Mirage 2000	Mirage IV	Mirage III; Mirage F-1; Noratlas; E-2	Super Etendard; F-8 Crusader; Alizé; Atlantique; P-2	Broussard; Caravelle; DHC-6; DC-8; KC-135; Mystère: Noratlas; Nord 262; Paris; Transall C-160
Germany (360)	Alphajet; F-4; F-104; Tornado		F-4	Atlantique F-104; Tornado;	Transall C-160
India (530)	Ajeet (Gnat); Hunter; Jaguar; Marut; MiG-21; MiG-23; Mirage 2000; Su-7	Canberra; Jaguar	Canberra; MiG-25	Alize; Il-38; Sea Harrier; Sea Hawk; Super Constellation	An-12; An-32; Boeing 737; DHC-3; DHC-4; HS-748
Iran (362)	F-4; F-5; F-14		F-4	P-3	Aero Commander 690; C-130; F-27; Falcon 20
Iraq (335)	Hunter; MiG-21; MiG-23; Mirage F-1; Su-20	Il-28; Tu-22		Super Etendard	An-2; An-12; An-24; An-26; Heron; Il-14; Il-76; Il-124
Israel (480)	A-4; F-15; F-16; Kfir; Mirage III		Boeing 707; C-130; E-2; F-4; OV-1; U-21		Arava; Boeing 707; C-130; Islander; KC-130; KC-707
Italy (130)	F-104; G-91; Tornado		F-104; G-91; G-222; PD-808	Atlantique	C-130; G-222
Japan (345)	F-1; F-4; F-15; F-104		F-4	E-2; P-2; PS-1; S-2	C-1; C-130; YS-11
Netherlands (126)	F-5; F-16; F-104		F-104	Atlantique; F-27; P-3	F-27
Pakistan (240)	Chinese A-5; F-16; MiG-19; Mirage III; Mirage 5		Mirage III	Atlantique	Bonanza; C-130; Falcon 20; F-27; L-100; Super King Air
Saudi Arabia (95)	Lightning; F-5; F-15		E-3		Boeing 747; C-130; C-212; Jetstar; KC-135
Spain (115)	F-4; F-5; Mirage III; Mirage F-1		HA-220	AV-8A Matador (Sea Harrier); P-3	Azor; CASA-207; C-130; C-212; DHC-4; Do-27; KC-130
Sweden (370)	J-35 Draken; J-37 Viggen; Saab 105		S-37 Viggen		Caravelle; C-47; C-130
Switzerland (360)	F-5; Hunter; Mirage III; Venom		Mirage III; Venom		
Syria (420)	MiG-17; MiG-21; MiG-23; MiG-25; Su-7; Su-20				An-24; An-22; Il-14; Il-18; Il-72; Mystère 20
USSR and Warsaw Pact generally (4,850)	MiG-21; MiG-23; MiG-25; MiG-27; MiG-29; Su-7; Su-15; Su-17; Su-24; Su-25; Su-27; Tu-28; Yak-28	M-4; Tu-16; Tu-22; Tu-22M; Tu-95	MiG-21; MiG-25; Tu-16; Tu-22; Tu-95; Tu-126; Su-17; Yak-28	An-12; Tu-16; Tu-22; Tu-22M; Tu-95; Su-17; Yak-36	An-12; An-22; An-24; An-26; Il-14; Il-18; Il-76
Turkey (250)	F-4; F-5; F-100; F-104		F-5	S-2	C-47; C-130; C-160
United Kingdom (348)	Buccaneer; Harrier; Hawk; Jaguar; Lightning; Phantom; Tornado		Jaguar; Nimrod; Shackleton	Nimrod; Sea Harrier	C-130; VC-10; Victor
United States (2,200)	A-10; F-4; F-14; F-15; F-16; F-111	B-1B; B-52; FB-111	C-135; E-2; E-3; E-4; E-6; F-4; OV-10; SR-71; TR-1; U-2	A-4; A-6; AV-8 (Sea Harrier); F-4; F-14; F-18; E-3; P-3; S-3	C-5; C-130; C-141; KC-135

Glossary

Aerodynamics The study of air and gases in motion and their mechanical effects, especially on flight.

After-burner A method of providing increased thrust to a jet engine through a nozzle at the rear, which reignites the hot gases and adds additional fuel. Also known as "Reheat."

Airborne Early Warning (AEW) The use of radar equipped aircraft to provide early warning of approaching enemy aircraft and missiles.

Air-to-Air Missile (AAM) A missile launched from an aircraft in the air and designed to knock out airborne aircraft or missiles.

Air-to-Surface Missile (ASM) A missile fired from the air against ground or sea targets.

Area Defense Anti-aircraft defenses designed to protect an area of ground or group of ships at sea.

Avionics The electronic systems used in an aircraft.

Camber The shape of the cross-section of a wing.

Canard Small wing, like a tailplane, mounted in front of the main aircraft wings to reduce drag.

Chaff Metallic strips used to confuse radar guided missiles. It was used in World War II, when it was known as "Window" and designed to confuse ground radars.

Combat Radius The distance that an aircraft can fly from its base and still have sufficient fuel left to return.

Control Column The pilot's main means of controlling his aircraft. It used to be called the "joystick."

Control Surfaces Movable parts of the wings and tailplane, which enable the aircraft to fly and maneuver.

Counter-air Operations by an air force against an enemy force.

Dash Range An aircraft's range flying at maximum speed.

Dumb Bomb An unguided bomb.

Electronic Counter Measures (ECM) Methods used to protect an aircraft from electronic detection or electronically guided attack.

Electronic Counter Counter Measure (ECCM) Electronic methods or overcoming the enemy's ECM.

Fire and Forget A missile which finds its own way to the target without having to be guided there by the operator.

Flight Profile A means of describing how an aircraft carries out a mission, whether at high or low level.

Fly-by-wire The use of electronic circuits to operate the control surfaces.

Head Down Display Cockpit instruments which enable the pilot to fly blind without looking out of his cockpit.

Head Up Display Luminous display of data in the cockpit window, which enables a pilot to engage a target without taking his eyes off it to check the cockpit instruments.

Identification Friend or Foe (IFF) An electronic device for checking whether an aircraft is friendly.

Loiter An aircraft cruising in a particular area.

Mach A means of describing aircraft speed. Mach 1 is the speed of sound, which can vary with differences in air density, humidity and altitude, Mach 2, twice the speed of sound, etc.

Multi-Role An aircraft designed to carry out a range of different tasks.

Offensive Air Support Air operations in support of armies and fleets.

Payload The weight of weapons, supplies and personnel which an aircraft can carry.

Pitch Movement about an axis at right angles to the fuselage.

Point Defense Anti-aircraft defense of a particular vital point on land or an individual ship at sea.

Pod A container mounted underneath an aircraft which contains weapons or surveillance systems.

Range The distance between two points which an aircraft can fly without refueling. Often known as "ferry range."

Reheat See After-burner.

Roll Movement of an aircraft about an axis running the length of the fuselage.

Sideways Looking Airborne Radar (SLAR) A radar which looks sideways, as opposed to forward or downward.

Smart Bomb A bomb which is guided onto its target.

Sonobuoy A device which is dropped into the sea to listen for submarines. Used passively, it cannot identify range or direction, but cannot be located by the submarine. If it sends out signals, it can pinpoint a submarine, but can also be detected by the latter.

Subsonic Below the speed of sound.

Supersonic Above the speed of sound.

Surface-to-Air (SAM) Ground or ship launched missiles designed to destroy aircraft or missiles.

Variable Geometry The ability to alter the sweep of the wings while in flight.

Variant Structural alterations to a basic aircraft to fit it for a particular role or roles.

Yaw Movement of an aircraft about a vertical axis going down through the center of the fuselage.

Index

PRINTED IN BELGIUM BY

INTERNATIONAL BOOK PRODUCTION